HAVE YOU EVER WONDERED?

Whatever became of Wynne Gibson, star of early talkies who was often cast as "a tough blonde dame"? Or Phyllis Brooks, another lovely blonde of stage and screen? (She is married to a congressman, a former roommate of John F. Kennedy.) Did you ever know that Alice Marble, who became the world's greatest woman tennis player, never won an important tournament until she overheard Clark Gable saying she didn't have what it took to win? Or that "Crash Corrigan," the showman star of the Saturday matinee, did death-defying stunts in 105 Westerns? Or that *My Friend Flicka*'s friend was John Washbrook? Or that John Bromfield, the sheriff of *Cochise* on TV, lives in a mobile park home?

THE NEW GIANT
LAMPARSKI'S
WHATEVER BECAME OF . . . ?

will thrill, chill and astonish all nostalgia fans who want to laugh, cry or merely shake their heads about the lives of yesteryear's great stars . . .

LAMPARSKI'S WHATEVER BECAME OF...?

RICHARD LAMPARSKI

BANTAM BOOKS · TORONTO · NEW YORK · LONDON

LAMPARSKI'S WHATEVER BECAME OF . . .?
A Bantam Book / November 1976

ISBN 0-553-10102-1

Published simultaneously in the United States and Canada

Bantam Books are published by Bantam Books, Inc. Its trade-
mark, consisting of the words "Bantam Books" and the por-
trayal of a bantam, is registered in the United States Patent
Office and in other countries. Marca Registrada. Bantam
Books, Inc., 666 Fifth Avenue, New York, New York 10019.

PRINTED IN THE UNITED STATES OF AMERICA

0 9 8 7 6 5 4 3 2 1

This book of extraordinary people who are known to millions is dedicated to two who are known only to a fortunate few:

ARNOLD STIEFEL
and
MURIEL SHOPWIN-POLLIA

The author would like to express thanks to the following individuals and firms who helped in the preparation of this book:
Eddie Brandt's Saturday Matinee, John Scott Miller, The Blood-Horse, Anselma Dell'Olio, Malcom Leo, Wayne Clark, Jeanne Youngson, Cinemabilia, Don Koll, Dick Lynch, Don Miller, Jon Virzi, Diana Serra Cary, Jerry Mastroli, Movie Star News, Charles Higham, Leonard Maltin, George Eells, DeWitt Bodeen, Joe Olmos, Joseph O'Donohue IV, Chris Albertson, Tommy Cooper, Bob Chatterton, R.C. Perry, Helen Maizner, Brian Gari, Ed Dodson, Frank Buxton, Tim Doherty, Laos Chuman, Myron Braun, Peaches Poland, Joel Preisler, Glen Roven, Robin O'Hara, Bob Cushman, Dan Woodruff, Hollywood Poster Exchange, Kirk Alyn, Richard Hudson's Hollywood Revue.

A special thanks to Richard Schaeffer whose assistance enriched this book in so many ways.

Individuals whose names are footnoted (4 and 5) in the text appear as separate segments in previous volumes in this series. Footnote 4 refers to Whatever Became of . . . ? Fourth Series and footnote 5 refers to Whatever Became . . . ? Fifth Series. These books are available in hardcover by Crown Publishers and in paperback by Bantam Books.

ALICE MARBLE

The woman who in 1964 was named to the
Tennis Hall of Fame was born on a farm near
Beckwourth, California on September 28,
1913. Before turning to tennis when she was fifteen years old, Alice made quite a name for herself locally as a baseball player.

The late Eleanor Tennant, who had been a
national ranking player, saw Alice's potential
and became her coach and manager. By 1931
she had taken the California Junior Tennis

Championship. Then she won the National Girls Doubles and narrowly missed winning the Singles. By 1932 she ranked Number Seven in the country and a year later she was Number Three.

Then serious illness took her off the courts. Doctors told her she could never again play tennis and probably would not live to be twenty-five years old. But by 1937 Alice was not only back but she took the Wimbledon Mixed Doubles, a feat she repeated in 1938. Some of her other victories were in the National Singles in 1938 and 1939 and the National Doubles the same years.

A remark by Clark Gable about her game which Alice overheard was the turning point in her career on the courts.

1939 was the year of Alice Marble. She won all six major championships, a feat without precedent. No woman has ever matched that record. She was on the Best Dressed list and named one of the Ten Most Outstanding Women in America. Her cannonball smash service had made her world famous.

In 1940 Alice turned professional and spent two very profitable seasons on tour. The money she earned was shrewdly invested for her by her close friend, the late Will du Pont.

She was among the first to wear smartly tailored shorts instead of billowing skirts on the court. The tennis togs she designed were carried by Saks Fifth Avenue. There was the Alice Marble racket, which she built and marketed. She sang in smart supper clubs and was for a while a sportscaster over New York radio station WNEW. Alice was as much a part of the Hollywood social swim as any movie star.

She shares a house at the Palm Desert Country Club with a Siamese cat. Her only husband was killed in action three weeks before V-E Day. They had been married only three years. She writes an occasional newspaper article and acts as Social Director at her club. Since her eyes began to trouble her she has played very little tennis, but spends a lot of time on the golf course. Although she has only one lung, Alice smokes and drinks.

The woman who took the championship away from Helen Hull Jacobs and trained the late Maureen Connolly rates Jadwiga Jedrzejowska, who beat her five times running, as her toughest opponent. She considers Billie Jean King as her only failure. Says Alice, who coached Ms. King, "She lacks the graciousness that makes a great champion."

Alice and Efrem Zimbalist, Jr. were received at Pickfair by Mary Pickford in 1963.

The turning point of her career came just before the game that made her eligible for Wimbledon. She overheard Clark Gable remark to her closest friend, Carole Lombard—"Let's face it. Alice just doesn't have what it takes to win at a really important tournament." Says Alice: "Clark was right. Until that moment I did lack the drive to win big. But hearing him say that made me so mad I went out on that court and gave that poor girl the beating of her life. I never played again that I wasn't determined to prove him wrong."

Eleanor Roosevelt joins Alice in opening Navy Relief Fund Drive.

Alice's home, which she shares with a Siamese cat, is on the grounds of the Palm Desert Country Club, where she is a Social Director. (Lauren Eason)

HIGHLIGHTS

1913   Born September 28 on a California farm

1931   Wins California Junior National Girls Doubles

1933   She ranked 3rd in the U.S.

1938   Wins Wimbledon Mixed Doubles for second time

1939   Wins all 6 major championships; named one of Ten Best Dressed Women and one of the Ten Most Admired Women in America

1940   Turned professional

Rod played "Bitter Creek" Yauntis in the 1948 western *Belle Starr's Daughter*.

ROD CAMERON

The stalwart leading man of movies and TV was born Ron Cox in Calgary, Alberta, Canada on December 7, 1912.

Cameron was in his early twenties when he came to New York City in the depths of the Great Depression to work as a sandhog. The same job brought him to Southern California, where he helped dig the waterway which brought water from the Colorado River to the Los Angeles area.

Rod tried his luck in movies not to fulfill a desire to act, but because he had heard "there was good money to be made in pictures." He had the looks which at the time were considered to be very desirable. He was "tall, dark and handsome."

He began making the rounds of casting offices. While waiting to get a real part in a film he was a stand-in for Fred MacMurray and doubled for Buck Jones in the serial *Riders of Death Valley* (1941). He managed to get a Screen Actors Guild card when the director Edmund Goulding gave him a small role in *The Old Maid* (1939) which was edited out of the final print.

Two of his other small parts were in *The Night of January 16th* (1941) with Nils Asther[5] and *True to the Army* (1942) with Allan Jones[4] and Judy Canova. Then a screen test he made for Columbia Pictures got him a contract with Paramount. Ironically, his first lead was playing a sandhog in *No Time for Love* (1943). The star of the picture was Claudette Colbert (widowed and living on Barbados).

After that he made *Gung Ho!*, the tongue-in-cheek western *Frontier Gal* (1945) with Fuzzy Knight (living in Hollywood), *The Runaround* (1946) with Ella Raines (living with her husband, a retired Air Force General, in Steamboat Springs, Colorado), *Stampede* (1949) with the late Johnny Mack Brown, *Dakota Lil* (1950) with Marion Martin (married to a doctor and living in Santa Monica), *Stage to Tucson* (1951) with Sally Eilers[4] and *Commandos Strike at Dawn* (1954).

9

Cameron's only really big part in an "A" picture was opposite Yvonne De Carlo in *Salome, Where She Danced* in 1945.

For the remainder of the fifties he was busy on television, starring in his three series, *City Detective* from 1953 to 1955, *State Trooper* from 1957 to 1959 and *Coronado 9* from 1959 to 1960. *Surfside Six*, which was on network TV from 1960 to 1962, gave him the greatest exposure of his career, but he has been relatively inactive since then.

While he never rose above the two-dimensional hero, he was very popular with Saturday matinee audiences in western and slam-bang serials such as *The Secret Service in Darkest Africa* (1942).

Cameron had contracts with Paramount, Universal, Fox, Columbia and Republic. At the latter his original agreement stipulated that he would not be assigned a picture opposite Vera Hruba Ralston,⁴ who was then the queen of the lot and the wife of its president. But when his option came up, his agent forgot the clause. He was immediately cast in two of her vehicles: *Spoilers of the Forest* (1957) and *The Man who Died Twice* (1958), Ms. Ralston's swan song.

Rod's screen image of the straight, no-nonsense outdoorsman was somewhat at odds with his personal life. He has a daughter by his first marriage which ended in divorce after he became successful. He was wed briefly to Marie Winsor. During his four-year marriage to Portuguese actress Angela Alves-Lico he was arrested for drunk driving. Almost as soon as their divorce became final in 1954, he stunned Hollywood by marrying the mother of his third wife. There was also a paternity suit at the height of his career.

The Camerons live in a large home in Granada Hills, California, with Rod's son Tony, who is his wife's grandson, and his former mother-in-law.

HIGHLIGHTS IN THE LIFE OF ROD CAMERON

1912 Born Dec. 7 in Calgary, Alberta, Canada

1939 Broke into movies in *The Old Maid*

1943 Big career break opposite Claudette Colbert in *No Time for Love*

1945 Made his most important film, *Salome, Where She Danced*

1953-62 Featured in four successful TV series

1954 Married for the fourth time—to the mother of his third wife

---

Los Angeles Times ★9 A.M. FINAL

FILM ACTORS SEIZED IN NARCOTICS RAID

Robert Mitchum Faces Marijuana Count With Lila Leeds, Two Others

Actor Robert Mitchum, Actress Lila Leeds and two companions were arrested last night on suspicion of violating the narcotics laws.

The four were arrested at a house rented by Miss Leeds at 8443 Redpath Drive in Hollywood. Both couples freely admitted to possession and use of marijuana cigarettes, Federal and city narcotics officers reported.

LILA LEEDS

The starlet who was arrested along with Robert Mitchum for possession of marijuana was born Lila Lee Wilkinson on January 28, 1928, in Dodge City, Kansas. She says her great uncle is former Postmaster General James Farley.

Lila in prison cell.

While in high school in Clovis, New Mexico, Lila was voted "Miss Clovis." The late dress designer Howard Greer brought her to Hollywood as a model. She began dating such celebrities as Jackie Coogan and Orson Welles and was appearing in a little theatre production when MGM signed her to a term contract. After small parts in *Green Dolphin Street* and *The Lady in the Lake* in 1947, she was dropped.

Even before coming to Hollywood, Lila had smoked marijuana. She was first turned on in St. Louis by members of the Stan Kenton band. After leaving Metro she was signed by Warner Brothers. The studio fired her, however, when she and a male star were discovered smoking pot behind a set. When she did well in *Moonrise* (1948) for Republic, Warners brought her back with a new contract and a raise.

Lila had first met Robert Mitchum at the Marion Davies beach house. She did not know him well when they were arrested together in her home on September 1, 1948. She has never seen or heard from him since. Around Hollywood their arrest was generally thought to have been a frame-up by the police, who needed a big-name drug raid to offset their growing reputation for corruption. Ironically, it only helped Mitchum's career. His studio, RKO, rushed his three completed features into release. The headlines had made him "hot" at the box office. Lila was on the wrong side of Hollywood's double standard. Warners dropped her immediately. The only work she could get after that was the exploitation cheapie *Wild Weed* (1949).

Soon after serving her 50-day jail sentence for the pot charge she took an overdose of sleeping pills. In 1949, a judge barred her from California for five years after a reckless driving arrest. A naval officer sued her for the return of a $1,000 ring. In 1954 she was arrested on a hard drug charge. Two years later she was sent to prison for prostitution. In 1961, Lila brought a paternity suit against the son of Jake Avery, the Chicago political boss.

Lila, who is now single, has been divorced three times. She is the mother of two sons and a daughter.

She told an interviewer recently that even when she was a heroin addict she spent a lot of time in churches. When she was seventeen

To Richard God be with you always Lila Leeds

years old, she says, she had a vision of Jesus. In 1967, a year after she gave up narcotics, she "heard bells" and felt she was "being called." Since 1973 Lila has been an ordained minister of a spiritualist church only two blocks away from Paramount Studios in Hollywood. She hopes her friends from the old days will help her to give former drug addicts a new start. The corporate name of her church, thrift shop and rehabilitation center is S.M.I.L.E.

HIGHLIGHTS IN THE LIFE OF LILA LEEDS

1928 Born Jan. 28 in Dodge City, Kansas

1945 Came to Hollywood to model

1946 Signed to MGM contract

1948 Arrested with Robert Mitchum on marijuana charge

1949 Barred from state of California

1954 Arrested on drug charge

1956 Sentenced to prison for prostitution

1961 Files paternity suit against Jake Avery's son

1967 "Heard bells" and felt she was "being called" to a religious vocation

1973 Founded spiritualist church in Hollywood

Charmain Carr, Nicholas Hammond, Heather Menzies, Duane Chase, Angela Cartwright, Debbie Turner and Kym Karath.

THE CHILDREN IN
THE SOUND OF MUSIC

When Twentieth Century Fox in 1965 released *The Sound of Music*, it was a studio torn by warring executive factions, facing a possible proxy fight and in serious financial trouble. Movie musicals at the time were thought to be "out." The film version of the Rodgers and Hammerstein Broadway hit received so-so to poor notices. Its sole star was Julie Andrews. Her stock had risen during the film's production when her picture *Mary Poppins* became a box-office smash of 1964. When she was signed for *The Sound of Music*, the seven young actors who were to play her step-children had never even heard of her. Neither had most movie goers.

"Kurt"—Duane Chase—is a student of Geology at the University of California in Santa Barbara. (Michael Knowles)

Duane Chase, the mischievous "Kurt," is still recognized a lot. Like most of his movie family, he received merciless teasing by his classmates after the picture was released. Now very few of his friends even know he has acted. He is a geology major at the University of California in Santa Barbara.

"Louisa," Heather Menzies, was for a long while a close friend of Charmain Carr and Angela Cartwright, but seldom sees them anymore. Like Charmain, *The Sound of Music* was her very first audition and her acting debut. She had a running part on *The Farmer's Daughter* on TV and has been in the movies *How Sweet It Is* (1968) and *Sssssss* (1973). She lives in the Hollywood Hills with an actor.

Debbie Turner, who was "Marta," says she doesn't remember much about making the picture. The only other acting she did before or since the movie was in commercials. A psychology major at USC, she doesn't plan to act again and feels she was not very good in the picture.

"Gretl"—Kym Karath—acts occasionally on TV and attends college in Los Angeles. (Brian De Palma)

Kym Karath, who played the youngest, "Gretl," had made several features before *The Sound of Music* and has remained active since on such TV shows as *The Brady Bunch* and *The Waltons*. Although her parents are very anxious for her to succeed in movies, Kym feels she may decide to pursue a different career. She attends a private school in Los Angeles.

"Louisa"—Heather Menzies—lives with another actor in the Hollywood Hills. (Claude Stiefel)

"Marta"—Debbie Turner—is a Psychology student at USC. (Jimmy Eason)

By the tenth anniversary of the film's opening it had earned $83,891,000 in the United States alone and had saved its studio from bankruptcy. It won five Academy Awards, including one for Best Picture of the Year, and its sound track album had become the third largest seller of all time. Exhibitors reported that many people came to see the blockbuster again and again. One woman in Scotland claimed to have sat through it almost 300 times.

For the seven unknowns who portrayed the motherless children, the experience of making the picture was a very happy one. It did not, however, make any one of them a star and several feel it probably lost them other important roles. For all its popularity, there are many in film circles who dismiss the picture as a schmaltzy fluke.

Charmain Carr, who played the oldest of the Von Trapp children, "Liesl," is married to a dentist and lives in Encino, California. She lost an important part in the TV series *Peyton Place* because of her screen image forged in *The Sound of Music*. She and her husband have an agreement which permits her to act only in commercials. They fear that a more active career might interfere with the raising of their two children. She is still close to Nicholas Hammond, who played her oldest brother, "Friedrich."

Hammond, who celebrated his fourteenth birthday during the filming, had had some prior stage experience. He quit acting while in college for four years but since then has had roles in the films *Skyjacked* (1972) and *Superdad* (1973). He is single and lives in Santa Monica.

Although Charmain Carr "Liesl" is married and a mother, she and Nicholas Hammond, "Friedrich" are still good friends. (Lauren Eason)

Angela Cartwright, who was "Brigitta," continued at Fox for three years in the TV series *Lost in Space*. She also played a daughter to Danny Thomas on his television show for seven years. She shares a San Fernando Valley apartment with an actor.

"Brigitta"—Angela Cartwright—is an actress and model living in North Hollywood. (Mary Cary)

The only Von Trapp the seven ever met was Maria, who now runs a ski lodge in Stowe, Vermont. None of them was paid much more than Screen Actors Guild minimum for their parts in the picture that became the biggest money-maker in the history of Twentieth Century Fox. It is second only to *The Godfather* as the largest grosser in the history of motion pictures.

They have all seen the film many times and loved it. They all liked Julie Andrews.

Julie Andrews and Christopher Plummer with the children from *The Sound of Music*.

Highlights of *Sound of Music*

1965   Movie version of musical is released. Wins five Oscars.

1970   Re-released to smash business.

1975   Has earned $83,891,000.00. Record album is third largest seller in history.

JANE GREER

Jane Greer was LIFE magazine's cover story on June 2, 1947.

The sultry siren of the screen was born a fraternal twin in Washington, D.C. on September 9, 1924. Her father invented gadgets, such as an onion peeler. Her mother, who was very ambitious for Jane, wrote poetry.

Jane was singing in the capitol with the Eric Madriguera Orchestra at the swank Del Rio Club when her mother, who worked for the War Department, arranged for her to be photographed by LIFE wearing the first WAC uniform. Three movie studios tested her after seeing the photo.

Paramount promised her a term contract, but after she had packed and been given a farewell party, the studio reneged. Shortly after that, Howard Hughes put her under personal contract, although it was six months before she even met him. The first thing he did was order her to stop dating Rudy Vallee. Instead, she married the singer, who was twenty-three years her senior. Six months later, in July of 1944, they filed for divorce.

After leaving Vallee, Jane began dating Hughes, but since he had still not put her in a picture, she secured her release. She went then to RKO, where she remained until the completion of *The Company She Keeps* (1950). The only reason she left then was that Hughes had taken over the lot and was giving all the plum parts and publicity to Jane Russell and Faith Domergue.

Probably her two best pictures were *They Won't Believe Me* (1947), her personal favorite, and *Out of the Past* (1947). The latter is considered by some cinema cultists as the ultimate film noir. She is still friendly with Robert Mitchum, her co-star in it.

Some of her other movies were: *George White Scandals* (1945) with Ethel Smith[3], *Station West* (1948), *The Big Steal* (1949) with the late Ramon Navarro[1] and *The Prisoner of Zenda* (1952).

Jane was teamed with Peter Lawford in the 1952 MGM production *You for Me*.

Jane with leading man Gary Cooper in *You're In the Navy Now*.

After *Down Among the Sheltering Palms* (1953), she took some time off to spend with her husband, producer Edward Lasker, the son of Albert Lasker, the "father of modern advertising."

She returned for *Run for the Sun* (1956) and *Man of a Thousand Faces* (1957) with Jeanne Cagney (single and living in Newport Beach, California). Then she disappeared again until *Where Love Has Gone* (1964). By then Jane had been divorced and was devoting all her time to her three sons.

She was disappointed when the role in *Bedlam* that she wanted so much went to Anna Lee. Henry Hathaway, who directed her as Gary Cooper's wife in *You're In the Army Now*

(1951) was the only person she really disliked working with.

Jane Greer enjoyed great personal popularity at RKO. She was easy to work with and had a well-deserved reputation for intelligence and wit. An offhand remark she made over twenty years ago is still quoted by show business wags. In it she gave Freddie Brisson, the producer and husband of Rosalind Russell, a highly uncomplimentary name that haunts him to this day. The Brissons have remained unamused by her remark, a play on the title, *Wizard of Oz*.

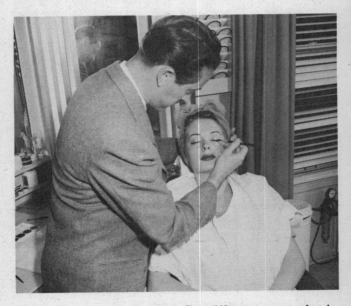

Famed movie make-up artist Perc Westmore puts finishing touches on Jane before a shooting.

Her lovely face made LIFE's cover on June 2, 1947. Her unique screen presence won her a place along with Liz Taylor and Ava Gardner in a 1949 press poll as one of the screen's top female stars.

She has fond recollections of her career but no wish to resume acting full time. Her cameo in the feature, *The Outfit* (1974) and a part on the TV series *Colombo* in 1975 satisfied her desire to perform now and then. Much of her spare time is spent working for the charity SHARE.

Jane lives in Bel-Air, California, with her poodle, two goats, two parrots and an actor. (Anselma Dell'Olio)

MILESTONES

1924 Born September 9 in Washington, D.C.

1942 Modeled the first WAC uniform in LIFE

1943 Signed a personal contract with Howard Hughes

1944 Married and divorced Rudy Vallee

1947 Made LIFE's cover

1949 Named one of the 10 Top Female Stars

1950 Leaves RKO studios

1963 Divorced again. Begins semi-retirement

GENERAL CURTIS LE MAY

This photo released by the Air Force in 1957. The ever-present cigar was part of Le May's public posture of toughness. (UPI)

The controversial military leader and would-be politician was born in Columbus, Ohio on November 15, 1906. He was in the ROTC at Ohio State University, where he earned a civil engineering degree. He entered the Army in 1928 as a 2nd Lieutenant.

Le May had been flying fighter planes for seven years when early in World War II he was chosen to pilot the first Flying Fortress. Even before he was promoted to Major General in 1943 he had the bearing of someone in total command. Although the men of lower rank may never have warmed to his burly, critical demeanor they were impressed by his courage under fire. His superiors considered him a boy wonder after the success of his B-17 raids over Germany. His "extraordinary heroism" was noted when he was awarded the Distinguished Service Cross.

In 1944 he was transferred to the China-Burma Theatre of war and proceeded to inspire his men with his iron will and sheer bluff against difficult odds. By V-J Day he had won the Silver Star.

He directed the daring air attack on Tokyo during which twenty-five hundred tons of incendiary bombs were dropped. LeMay took a major part in the planning of the atomic bombing of Hiroshima and Nagasaki.

Le May is generally credited with being the architect of the Berlin Airlift. During the years 1948 to 1957 while he was Chief of the Strategic Air Command, he was very outspoken on America's dealings with the Soviets. President Kennedy once assessed Le May thusly: "If you have to go you want Le May in the lead bomber. But you never want Le May deciding whether or not you have to go."

Many guessed it was Le May being lampooned by George C. Scott in the 1964 film *Dr.*

Strangelove, or: How I Learned to Stop Worrying and Love the Bomb.

As Air Force Chief of Staff from 1962 to 1965, the General lobbied actively for more sophisticated nuclear weapons which he considers "nothing more than another kind of armament in our arsenal." His constant clashes with Defense Secretary Robert McNamara earned him much publicity and many admirers.

Time magazine featured the American Independent candidate in its cover story of October 18, 1968. The pair ended up receiving 13.2% of the total votes cast.

Governor Wallace chose Le May as his running mate in 1968 in hopes of attracting voters in Ohio and California.

Le May retired in 1965 and settled down to a $50,000-a-year job with an electronics company. As a hero of the Right Wing he was by no means out of the limelight, and by 1968 he brought out a book, *America is in Danger.*

What may have looked at the time to be an honor and opportunity proved to be his undoing. In 1968 Presidential candidate Governor George Wallace chose him to run as Vice President on the American Independent Party ticket. From their first public appearance together and throughout the campaign, Le May proved an embarrassment. He admitted that under some circumstances he could foresee the use of nuclear weapons. Another of his statements mentioned the possibility of bombing North Viet Nam "back into the Stone Age." The Wallace camp soon wished their first choice for a running mate had accepted. The number-two spot on the ticket went to Le May only after it had been turned down by "Colonel" Harlan Sanders of fried chicken fame.

Le May and Wallace confer during the last days of the 1968 campaign. 9,906,473 people voted for them, giving their ticket 46 electoral votes. (UPI)

Le May still does occasional consultation work, although flare-ups of his heart condition limit his activities mainly to hunting and fishing trips in his camper. He and his wife, who have one daughter, live in a modern home in Newport Beach, California. Two glass-front cabinets in the house are filled with his military decorations, including the Order of the Patriotic War from the Soviet Union.

General Le May leaves his Newport Beach, California home for frequent fishing and hunting trips with his wife. (Shelly Ramsdell)

MILESTONES IN THE LIFE OF CURTIS LE MAY

1906 Born November 15 in Columbus, Ohio

1928 Enters Army as 2nd Lieutenant

1943 Becomes first to pilot a Flying Fortress

1945 Awarded the Silver Star

1948-57 Chief of Strategic Air Command

1962-65 Air Force Chief of Staff

1965 Retires from Army

1968 Runs as George Wallace's Vice-Presidential candidate on American-Independent Party ticket

"BUCKWHEAT"

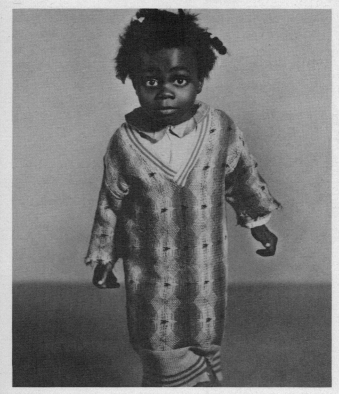

One of *Our Gang*'s most popular members was born William Thomas in Los Angeles on March 12, 1931. He is an only child. When he was three and a half years old, his mother heard that producer Hal Roach was looking for a replacement for "Stymie,"[5] who was getting too mature to take part in the mischief-making in the famous shorts. Out of hundreds of kids, Roach picked William.

A scene from the 1940 *Our Gang* comedy *Waldo's Last Stand* with Mickey Gubitosi (now a star under the name Robert Blake), Spanky McFarland, Darla Hood, the late Alfalfa and Buckwheat.

Thomas was added to the cast as "Buckwheat" in 1934. For the first few years William played the role as a little girl. His specialty of crying was particularly effective in diapers or a little dress. Surrounded by some of the cutest children ever in movies, "Buckwheat" was a standout.

Most of William's earnings were placed in trust for him by the court. His father was a janitor. His mother also received a salary for being with him at all times on the set and when the cast toured presentation houses all over the United States. Thomas feels he was well paid for the 78 comedies he appeared in.

Although he has only the happiest memories of *Our Gang*, Thomas has not kept in touch with anyone except "Stymie." They have remained close friends over the years and still see each other about once a week. The only sour note from his career came when it ended and he could no longer attend the studio school. He still cringes a little when he recalls how the other kids at public school teased him for the first few years.

When the *Our Gang* series was cancelled in 1944, William's career in film ended too—as an actor. Since leaving the U.S. Army after the Korean War, "Buckwheat" has been a film lab technician. He works at Technicolor in Holly-

A birthday celebration with Darla and Alfalfa.

wood. Says Thomas today: "I just couldn't see going from studio to studio auditioning, and I knew even the big names had to go through that. It seemed like too much of a rat race."

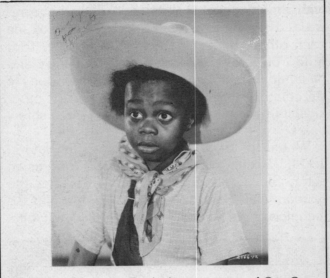

For the first few years Buckwheat was part of *Our Gang*, he played a little girl.

"Buckwheat's" friends and co-workers don't make a big thing about his background and his son, who is now in his twenties, has gotten used to the fact that his dad was once famous. He is, however, a hero among the youngsters in his neighborhood, who watch his pictures on TV under the title, *The Little Rascals*.

From time to time Thomas has been offered roles in movies, but he was never for a minute tempted to return to acting. He owns his own home, which is filled with ham radio equipment, and drives a late-model Cadillac. A divorcé, William was asked recently if the young women he dates are aware that he is "Buckwheat." The former child actor replied with a big, roguish grin, "Let us say that they are very impressed!"

HIGHLIGHTS

1931 Born March 21st in Los Angeles

1934 Chosen to replace "Stymie" in "Our Gang" shorts

1944 Movie career ends with cancellation of series

1953 Released from U.S. Army. Joins Technicolor

PAULINE STARKE

Pauline was loaned to First National Pictures by her home lot, MGM, to play opposite Ben Lyon in *The Perfect Sap* (1927).

The star of silent pictures was born in Joplin, Missouri, on January 10, 1901. After divorcing Pauline's father, Mrs. Starke was forced to support herself and her daughter. To escape the strong disapproval of their community, they came to Los Angeles, where her mother managed to get some work as a movie extra.

One day D.W. Griffith spotted Pauline standing on the sidelines watching her mother, who was part of a ballroom scene. The director brought the teenager into the sequence and placed her next to the star, Henry B. Walthall. When he saw how well she photographed, he immediately gave her a contract.

After appearing in Griffith's *Intolerance* (1916), she had her first lead in *Until They Get Me* (1917). By the following year, she was starring in such films as *Innocent's Progress*. Pauline was now making enough money to support her mother and grandmother.

When the late Mae Murray refused *Women Love Diamonds* (1927), Pauline was cast in the part opposite a very young Douglas Fairbanks, Jr.

Some of her more important features were *A Connecticut Yankee in King Arthur's Court* (1921), *In the Palace of the King* (1923) with Blanche Sweet[1] and Aileen Pringle,[2] *Dante's Inferno* (1924) and *The Man Without a Country* (1925).

The public first saw her as a blonde in the 1928 Technicolor feature, *The Viking*. The film had sound effects and a musical score.

She cried with such ease that directors cast her as the brow-beaten charlady and factory worker or a put-upon stenographer. The *Motion Picture Magazine* of November, 1921, called her "The Glad-Sad Girl." Pauline told them she was glad to play the sad parts. She was just happy to be in movies.

Soldiers of Fortune (1924) finally presented her as the beauty she was, and from then on her roles were more glamorous.

She had a reputation for being easy to work with and for taking direction without a fuss. It was, therefore, quite a surprise when she left her studio, MGM, in 1929. Only two years before, she had accepted the role in *Women Love Diamonds,* which Mae Murray had refused. It is still her personal favorite and was one of her biggest hits.

Pauline refuses to discuss the circumstances of the break. All she will say is "It was something very personal and caused me a great deal of unhappiness. They did their best to blackball me afterwards."

She managed to get some work in talkies but not enough to sustain her as a star. She made *Royal Romance* (1930) with William Collier, Jr. (living in San Francisco) for Columbia, and when Mary Nolan became temperamental on *What Men Want* (1930), Pauline replaced her. Another severe blow came after she had been signed for the lead in *The Great Gabbo* (1929). After a few days of shooting, its director, James

Cruze, replaced her with his ex-wife, the late Betty Compson.[2] By 1935 she was reduced to appearing in the poverty-row production, *$20 a Week*. It was her last film.

Pauline starred on Broadway in *Zombie* in 1932. Two years later, she married the play's producer. Recently she explained her virtual disappearance from Hollywood in the mid-thirties: "I wanted to put my career and everything that reminded me of it far behind me. My husband and I lived in Europe until 1940. After that we made our home on a large sailboat, which we took around the world several times."

Her Santa Monica apartment is filled with the treasures she acquired during her years of travel. (Martitia Palmer)

Ill health made the childless couple settle down finally in Santa Monica. Their apartment is filled with the art they collected during their years of travel. Pauline neither sees nor hears from any of her contemporaries, although she has only nice things to say about all of them.

The mystery of her whereabouts for so many years has made her one of the most sought-after stars by autograph collectors. She commented recently: "For years I tried very hard to forget that I ever had anything to do with pictures. Now, many young people come to my door. They know my work and say such kind things. I had thought I was forgotten. I'm terribly thankful that they found me. I had no idea that anyone cared."

TRANSITIONS

1901　Born January 10 in Joplin, Missouri

1915　Began acting in movies for D.W. Griffith

1924　Screen image became more glamorous

1929　Left MGM. Was replaced in *The Great Gabbo*

1932　Starred in *Zombie* on Broadway

1935　Made her last picture, a cheapie. Retired

DOUGLASS DUMBRILLE

One of Hollywood's great heavies was born on October 13, 1889, in Hamilton, Ontario, Canada. Before joining a stock company at the age of sixteen, he worked as a bank clerk for a salary of $5.00 a week.

His career on stage was much more varied than in movies. Although he specialized in character roles, he also was leading man to Jeanne Eagels, with whom he toured in *Rain* in 1923. He was with Eva Le Gallienne in *Call of Life* (1925), Vivienne Segal[3] in *The Three Musketeers* (1928) and Judith Anderson in *As You Desire Me* (1930).

Douglass was the domineering uncle of Marguerite Chapman in the 1946 film, *Pardon my Past*. It was directed by Leslie Fenton, who is now an antique dealer in Carmel, California.

Dumbrille was brought to Hollywood because of the flair he showed for comedy in *Child of Manhattan* (1932) on Broadway, but in pictures the only times he inspired laughs they were at his own expense. He played the pompous foil to a number of comics, but is best remembered as a crooked sheriff, cruel potentate or choleric tycoon.

Although he considered his screen debut to be *His Woman* (1931), actually he had first been seen as a corrupt politician who denies women the right to vote in the silent *What 80,000,000 Women Want* (1916).

His chief interest in film acting was always money and he dismissed most of his screen appearances in low-budget fare such as: *Hi, Nellie!* (1934) with the late Glenda Farrell, and *Tell No Tales* (1939), directed by Leslie Fenton (now an antique dealer in Carmel, California) But in one "B", *The Mysterious Rider* (1938), he gave a moving performance in a sympathetic part.

His "A" efforts include *Naughty Marietta* (1935), *Peter Ibbetson* (1935), *Lives of a Bengal Lancer* (1935), *Kentucky* (1938) and *Road to Utopia* (1946). His favorite role was in De Mille's *The Ten Commandments* (1956), but he felt his best work was in *Mr. Deeds Goes to Town* (1936). Its director, Frank Capra, is a man Dumbrille admired very much. About some of the others he had been associated with, he was less complimentary and very frank. Of movie mogul Harry Cohn, Douglass said: "He was as crude and rude a man as I've ever known." He dismissed his contemporary Paul Muni as "one of the greatest bad actors of all times." But in his entire career, he said he had never encountered a more unprofessional player than Tammy Grimes. Her TV show in 1966 was his swan song.

In 1958, two years after the death of his wife of forty-seven years, he married the daughter of his old friend, Alan Mowbray. His new father-in-law took a rather dim view of the union because of the great age difference.

Dumbrille's friend and contemporary, Alan Mowbray, took a rather dim view of Douglass' marriage to his daughter because of their vast age difference. Mowbray died on March 25, 1969.

Dumbrille was the evil desert ruler who made things hot for Abbott and Costello in the 1944 screen comedy *Lost in a Harem.*

In his last interview, held shortly before he died on April 2, 1974, Dumbrille's recollections of his career were vivid and his anecdotes were colored by a sharp wit, which fans seldom saw in his movies. He had recently advised his grandson to go into a profession other than "this silly business of acting." His young wife joined in the story-telling to remark: "I tell all of Doug's fans that I've known him since I was a little girl and never once has he placed bamboo shoots under my fingernails."

Douglass Dumbrille and his wife. the daughter of Alan Mowbray. in a photo taken a few months before his death in 1974. (Michael Knowles)

Transitions

1889   Born on October 13 in Hamilton, Ontario, Canada

1905   Left job at a bank to act

1923   Toured U.S. with Jeanne Eagels in *Rain*

1930   Played in *As You Desire Me* with Judith Anderson on Broadway

1931   Debuted in talkies

1936   Had his best movie role in *Mr. Deeds Goes to Town*

1956   Acted in De Mille's *The Ten Commandments*, his favorite part
       His wife died after forty-seven years of marriage

1960   Married the daughter of his friend, Alan Mowbray

1966   Retired

1974   Died on April 2 in Los Angeles

SHEENA, QUEEN OF THE JUNGLE
IRISH McCALLA

The actress who played the first liberated woman on television was born and raised in Pawnee City, Nebraska. One of a family of eight children, Irish's birthday was Christmas, 1929. She left home for California when she was 17 years old "to escape the cold weather."

Irish McCalla got the role of *Sheena* when Anita Ekberg failed to show up to film the pilot.

After a succession of waitress jobs she went to work at Douglas Aircraft. She was terminated from all of these positions after slapping either a boss's or a customer's face. "Where I come from," says Irish, "pretty girls are not overlooked, but no one mauls them. I wasn't used to it, and I did not like it. I still don't."

A friend suggested she try modeling. She was popular as a pin-up right from the start. If the photographers were no more gallant than other men in Hollywood had been, at least she was being paid better. "And," adds Irish, "it was always a frontal approach, which I can handle." Ms. McCalla is five feet nine inches tall.

Anita Ekberg, who had just been named Miss Sweden, was first signed for the title role of *Sheena, Queen of the Jungle*, but failed to show up to film the pilot. A photographer friend suggested Irish, who was grateful for the chance to make $365 a week. She used the money to get a divorce from her husband, an insurance man. Her two little boys announced to their playmates that "Mommy is going to work in the jungle."

The program's locale was supposed to be Africa, but it was actually filmed in Mexico. Twenty-six half hours were made over a seven-month period in 1955 and 1956. Had they not all been in black and white, *Sheena* would probably still be in syndication.

Like the comic-strip character on which it was based, *Sheena* wore a leopard skin and spoke in pidgin English. She fought bravely and successfully against ivory poachers and white hunters.

Sheena, Queen of the Jungle was a show that brought dads together with their sons in front of the family television set.

The male regular on the series was Christian Drake, who was forever stumbling into trouble. The audience at home may have been relating to her as a sex object, but the scripts had *Sheena* very much in command. In a complete reversal of roles, it was *Sheena* who always came to Drake's rescue. She reserved most of her attention and affection for her constant companion, "Chim." She and the chimpanzee often held hands, making him the world's most envied ape. *Sheena* was a show that brought dads together with their sons in front of the family TV set.

Irish did a few features after *Sheena*, in which she played small parts: *She Demons* (1958), *The Beat Generation* (1959), *Five Branded Women* (1960) and *Hands of a Stranger* (1962).

Irish's picture was on the jacket of a record album called *Music for Big Game Hunters*.

She lives with her cat "Tondelayo" on the beach in Malibu. (Peter Schaeffer)

She received residuals only for the last thirteen episodes of the show. For years afterward, however, she commanded large fees for personal appearances.

Irish has been divorced from her second husband, an actor, since 1966. She lives in a guest house only a few yards from the Pacific Ocean in Malibu. She has no interest in acting again, and her only contact with Hollywood is the twice-monthly trip she makes there to teach art. She has been a successful painter for almost ten years and has had several one-woman shows. Three of her oils were borrowed from a gallery by Pat Nixon and hung in San Clemente while it was the Western White House.

The woman whose image still occupies the fantasy life of many American males often goes for days without even answering her phone. Her sole companion is her cat, "Tondelayo." Says *Sheena*, "I love to be all alone."

JOHN QUALEN

The distinguished character actor was born in Vancouver, B.C., on December 8, 1889. Since his father, who was a minister, moved from one congregation to another, John spent parts of his boyhood in Minnesota, Ontario, Iowa and Illinois. After winning a gold medal and a one-year scholarship to Northwestern University in an oratorical contest, Qualen made up his mind to be an actor. His deeply religious parents were appalled and threatened to disown him.

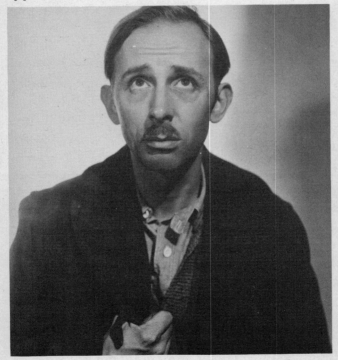

Broadway audiences first saw Qualen in *Street Scene* in 1929. He made his movie debut in the same role in 1931.

He acted in tent shows and stock companies until moving to New York City in 1928. The late playwright-director Elmer Rice chose him for the Broadway cast of *Street Scene* (1929), which was also his screen debut (1931). He was in Hollywood, filming *Arrowsmith* (1931), when Rice offered him a part in his play, *Counselor-at-Law* (1931). He returned to Hollywood for the movie version (1933) and has lived there ever since.

Qualen's paternal grandparents were from Norway and his mother was born there. Although he played Scandinavian characters many times, he always gave them more dimension than a stereotype. Norway showed its appreciation in 1946 when King Haakon VII honored him with a commemorative proclamation.

The only time he was under contract was for two years at Fox. During that time he played Papa Dionne in the three features the studio made about the world-famous Dionne Quintuplets,[3] beginning with *Country Doctor* (1936). After that, he was free to pick and choose the pictures that were offered to him.

Some of Hollywood's finest directors sought his services for some of their best films: Howard Hawks—*His Girl Friday* (1940); Michael Curtiz—*Casablanca* (1942), *Roughly Speaking* (1945); King Vidor[3]—*Our Daily Bread* (1934); William Wellman—*Nothing Sacred* (1937), *The High and the Mighty* (1954); John Ford—*The Grapes of Wrath* (1940), *The Long Voyage*

Home (1940), *The Fugitive* (1947), *The Man Who Shot Liberty Valance* (1962).

Some of his other appearances were in: *Thunder in the Night* (1935) with Karen Morley (the actress whose career was ruined by the Hollywood Blacklist, now Mrs. Lloyd Goff of Encino), *She Had to Eat* (1937) with Jack Haley[3] and the late Rochelle Hudson,[3] *Arabian Nights* (1942) with Jon Hall,[3] *Swing Shift Maisie* (1943) with James Craig (a realtor in Huntington Beach, California), *River Gang* (1945) with Gloria Jean,[4] *Captain China* (1950) with John Payne,[3] *Hans Christian Andersen* (1952), *At Gunpoint* (1955) with Jack Lambert (living in Carmel, California), *The Big Land* (1957) with Julie Bishop (married to a Beverly Hills physician) and *North to Alaska* (1960).

John played Papa Dionne in the three features made about the famous quintuplets.

In his big scene from *His Girl Friday* (1940).

The only time he was ever uncomfortable before a camera was in the Jimmy Stewart-Simone Simon[2] version of *Seventh Heaven* (1937). He disagreed with but accepted Henry King's direction. The film flopped. He speaks wistfully of turning down director Jean Renoir, who offered a part but asked him to take a cut in salary. Qualen declined. The film was *The River*, which is now considered a classic. The only role he wanted very much and lost was in the movie version of *I Remember Mama*. It went to Edgar Bergen[2] and was supposed to launch him as a serious actor. It didn't.

John accepts a part still as a favor to an old friend or because it is one that offers him a challenge. Recently he has done *The Sons of Katie Elder* (1965), *A Big Hand for the Little Lady* (1966) and *Firecreek* (1968).

Most of Qualen's time is spent gardening, wood turning and bicycling. Since the death of his old friend, Walter Brennan, the only one he sees from his heyday is Pat O'Brien. He and his wife of over fifty years live in West Los Angeles, not far from Twentieth Century-Fox Studios. They have three daughters and ten grandchildren.

Qualen today posed in front of a painting of himself in character from his 1940 picture, *The Long Voyage Home.* (Bogart Christi)

MILESTONES

1889 Born on December 8 in Vancouver, B.C., Canada

1928 Left a stock company to come to New York City

1929 Chosen by Elmer Rice for his play, *Street Scene*

1931 Made movie debut in *Street Scene*

1936 Made first of three features with the Dionne Quintuplets

1946 Decorated by King Haakon VII of Norway

Dorothy made her screen debut in *Black Magic* (1929).

DOROTHY JORDAN

The star who almost became Fred Astaire's first screen dancing partner was born in Clarksville, Tennessee, on August 9, 1908. Her family, whose ancestors were among the first settlers of Virginia, frowned on her theatrical ambitions at first. But when she turned eighteen and left for New York City to study at the American Academy of Dramatic Arts, it was with their blessings and financial support.

The stage star Ona Munson encouraged her and helped Dorothy get small parts in *Garrick Gaieties* (1926) with Sterling Holloway and *Twinkle Twinkle* (1926). She was in *Treasure Girl* (1928) with Gertrude Lawrence and understudied Adele Astaire in *Funny Face* (1928). For a brief time she was a Chester Hale[4] girl at the Capitol Theatre, more because of her looks, however, than her dancing skills.

When sound came in, almost all the stars took singing and dancing lessons. In this photo, Dorothy and Anita Page[5] are flanked by Kolb and Dill, a popular vaudeville team of the period.

Dorothy was part of the rush of Broadway people to Hollywood at the advent of talkies. Ona Munson arranged for her to be screen tested by Fox, where she was placed under contract. Her picture debut was *Black Magic* (1929).

In less than two years she had moved to MGM, where she made the classic *Min and Bill* (1930) and *Hell Divers* (1931) with Clark Gable.

Joel McCrea, her leading man in *The Lost Squadron* (1932), introduced her to movie mogul Merian C. Cooper. Shortly after they married in 1933, he placed her under contract to the studio he headed, RKO. Cooper was all for her continuing her film career and bought several properties for her. Dorothy's performance in *Bondage* (1933) with the late Isabel Jewell had given her career a big boost. She was slated to be teamed with Fred Astaire in his film debut, *Flying Down to Rio*. When she became pregnant, Ginger Rogers took over the part. From that picture, Rogers and Astaire became major stars.

Dorothy has no regrets. Nor did she ever miss stardom. Once a mother, she lost all interest in her career. Her husband, who was for many years a major power in Hollywood, encouraged her to act again, but not until the mid-fifties, after her two daughters and son were raised, did she reappear on the screen. Dorothy had small parts in *The Sun Shines Bright* (1954) and *The Searchers* (1956). In the intervening years she turned down a contract with Columbia Pictures and the lead in a Raoul Walsh film. The only role that tempted her was that of "Melanie" in

Gone With the Wind, for which she tested.

Dorothy's husband had a military career which was as colorful and as successful as the one he had in Hollywood. He produced *This is Cinerama, The Quiet Man* and was co-director of *King Kong.* Their home in Coronado, California, is filled with mementos of his life.

In the early talkie, *In Gay Madrid* (1930), she was teamed with Ramon Novarro, the Latin lover of the silents. The two brothers who beat Novarro to death in 1968 are still in prison.

Dorothy today, next to a still from *King Kong*, which her late husband co-directed. (Nichla Palmer)

The screen beauty co-starred with Robert Montgomery, Lionel Barrymore, Will Rogers, the late Paul Lukas and William Haines[4]. Yet she does not discuss her career today with any real interest, nor is there any evidence in her home that she was once a star. Her only connections with Hollywood since she was widowed in 1973 are her continuing friendships with Fay Wray and Maureen O'Sullivan.

In her still heavy Southern drawl, Dorothy told an interviewer recently: "Even before I married, the long hours of movie-making had begun to wear on me. I realized then that I didn't have the driving ambition it takes to be a star. I think

I've enjoyed being Mrs. Merian C. Cooper much more than being Dorothy Jordan. And I just *love* being a grandmother!"

HIGHLIGHTS

1908   Born on August 9 in Clarksville, Tennessee

1926   Made Broadway debut in *Garrick Gaieties.*

1928   Understudied Adele Astaire in *Funny Face.*

1929   Debuted in movies in *Black Magic*

1933   Married movie mogul Merian C. Cooper

1933   Her film *Bondage* was a big hit

1933   Became pregnant and could not dance with Fred Astaire in his first film, *Flying Down to Rio*

1954   Made brief comeback in *The Sun Shines Bright*

RAY "CRASH" CORRIGAN

The stuntman-showman-star of the Saturday matinee was born in Milwaukee, Wisconsin, on Valentine's Day 1902. Much of his youth was spent in Denver. The Corrigans moved to Los Angeles in 1920.

Until he was twenty years old, Ray was troubled by a curvature of the spine. He says that Bernarr Macfadden, who was the most famous physical culturist of that time, corrected his condition and taught him the methods of developing a good physique. By 1930, Corrigan was running the gym at Metro-Goldwyn-Mayer studios, which was franchised to Macfadden.

In Chapter Six of the serial *Undersea Kingdom* (1936), Corrigan was tied to the "Juggernaut" by his enemy, the late Lon Chaney, Jr. The twelve episodes were edited into a feature, which is now shown on television under the title, *Sharad of Atlantis.*

One of the many stars he conditioned was Dolores Del Rio, whose husband was then the studio's set designer, Cedric Gibbons. It was Gibbons who suggested to Louis B. Mayer that Corrigan be used to do the stunt work in the *Tarzan* films. MGM had hired the family of circus aerialists, The Flying Codonas, at $5,000 a week, but none of them were big enough to double for Johnny Weissmuller. At that time the swimmer had not learned to swing from a rope.

Soon "Crash" had not only a good reputation as a stuntman but developed a side career working in pictures as a gorilla. Two of his many appearances in which he was usually billed simply as "Naba," were in the feature *Murder in the Private Car* (1934) with Una Merkel[3] and the Clyde Beatty serial *Darkest Africa* (1936).

His first break as an actor came playing a very campy Apollo in *The Nightlife of the Gods* (1935). He also doubled several times for Clark Gable and played one of the crew members in *Mutiny on the Bounty* (1935).

He came into his own in low-budget westerns. Corrigan was first one of *The Three Mesquiteers* in that series of twenty-four horse operas made at Republic. Ray played "Tucson," the late Max Terhune was "Lullaby" and Bob Livingston was "Stony." Livingston was later replaced by John Wayne. Then "Crash" starred in and co-produced *The Buckskin Rangers* and *The Range Busters*, two series for Monogram.

He also starred in some serials: *The Leathernecks Have Landed* (1935), *Undersea Kingdom* (1936), which was set in the lost land of Atlantis, and *The Painted Stallion* (1937) with Duncan Renaldo.[3]

Where Corrigan made his fortune was "Corriganville," a 1611-acre ranch he bought in 1937 for $10,000. Almost immediately he began renting it to movie companies for their outdoor sequences. A few of the hundreds of pictures that were made there were: *Fort Apache*, *Duel in the Sun* and *How the West Was Won*. *Lassie*, *Rin-Tin-Tin* and *The Cisco Kid* were among the many television shows that were shot there. Once in one week he grossed $11,000 on rentals alone.

Ray built western towns, waterfalls, a Spanish village and in 1950, "Corriganville" was opened to the public. With personal appearances by movie stars, staged gunfights and heavy advertising, Corrigan collected admissions from 3,000,000 people before he sold it in 1965.

His first wife was Miss Altoona, Pennsylvania. They met while he was on a personal appearance tour. She was ushering for $7.00 a week in the movie house where he was playing. Their divorce came after "Crash" crashed into her motel room, along with three private detectives he had hired. Los Angeles newspapers reported the details of the triangle—the wife, a man who had recently been fired from his job of foreman at "Corriganville" and the western hero. The former foreman sued Ray for $3,000,000 for defamation of character and filed a battery complaint against him.

In 1954, when their divorce was granted, the judge made the three Corrigan children wards of the court, stating that Mrs. Corrigan was "unfit" to have custody. He termed Ray's relationship with his two daughters as "most reprehensible." The ex-Mrs. Corrigan received $300,000 at that time but in 1965 when Bob Hope bought "Corriganville" for $2,800,000, she got half of that amount. She still lives with Ray's ex-foreman. He was the man who shot and killed Carl "Alfalfa" Switzer of *Our Gang* fame in 1959 over a debt of $35.00. The findings of the inquest were that the shooting was "in self defense."

In the 1930s and '40s, Corrigan starred in 105 westerns and was featured in many more.

In 1956, Corrigan married Elaine Dupont, who was for a time a leading lady in westerns. Their best man was Rory Calhoun. They were divorced in 1967 but are still friends.

"Crash" who neither drank nor smoked died of a heart attack in August, 1976. He had spent the last few years of his life sailing and fishing in the river near his mobile home in Brookings Harbor, Oregon. Almost no one in the area knew anything of his years in motion pictures.

The last years of Corrigan's life were spent in a mobile home in Oregon. (Richard Schaeffer)

Milestones

1902—Born on Valentine's Day in Milwaukee, Wisconsin

1920—His family moved to Los Angeles

1930—Became physical therapist to the stars at the Metro-Goldwyn-Mayer studio gym

1932—Began doing stunt work in *Tarzan* films

1935—Got his first featured role in *The Nightlife of the Gods*

1939—Began starring in westerns

1965—Sold *Corriganville*, a ranch he bought for $10,000, to Bob Hope for $2,800,000

Richard Lamparski was one of the guests at the large party Capitol Records gave Mrs. Miller when her album appeared on the best-seller charts in 1965.

MRS. MILLER

The middle-aged housewife who overnight became a singing sensation in the 1960s was born Elva Connes on October 5 in Joplin, Missouri. Until 1965, she lived quietly with her husband, a retired gentleman rancher, in the college town of Claremont, California.

The Millers, who had no children, raised a niece. After their ward had married and left their home, Mrs. Miller began recording sacred songs at a small studio in Hollywood. She had studied voice at Pomona College but had no ambition to sing professionally. Up until then, the only singing she had ever done was in church choirs.

Some of the tapes she had made were taken to Capitol Records. The initial response was negative. Then one producer felt that with her training in classical music, she might bring something different to pop songs. Mrs. Miller was less than enthusiastic but consented to record some of the current hits: "These Boots Are Made for Walking," "A Hard Day's Night" and "Downtown."

Her album was what is known in the record business as a "sleeper."

Her album, *Mrs. Miller's Greatest Hits*, became what is known in the record industry as a "sleeper." Looking for something unusual, disc jockeys across the nation found it in Mrs. Miller. Some of her renditions included whistling. In the lingo of the music business, "they had found a new sound."

TV hosts Mike Douglas, Ed Sullivan and Merv Griffin had her on their shows again and again. She was a hit in Viet Nam, where she went to entertain the troops. When the records caught on in England, too, the BBC had her fly to London for a special appearance on television. Many suspected she was a put-on. But no one who saw her perform failed to be amazed at the rapport she had with an audience. Mrs. Miller had one of the warmest and most genuine smiles in show business. She truly enjoyed singing, and the public enjoyed her.

There was a second album, but it didn't do nearly as well. Then, against her better judgment, Mrs. Miller allowed her managers to talk her into recording songs with lyrics she did not understand. She found out later that the words were contemporary jargon for drugs.

At her peak she played some of the best night clubs in the nation. Her records appeared on the charts right alongside the Beatles, Elvis Presley and the Rolling Stones. Mrs. Miller made a great deal of money—mostly for other people.

In an interview in 1966 at the height of her popularity, she spoke of her sudden success: "It came from out of the blue and if it ends tomorrow I'll be just fine. My feet are on the ground. My life was far from empty before it happened." She had just been given a large party attended by celebrities from every field. She allowed that the greatest thrill of her experience had been meeting Leonard Bernstein, one of her heroes.

Now a widow, Mrs. Miller lives in a high-rise apartment building in the Los Feliz section of Los Angeles. She is frequently recognized at the many plays and concerts she attends. "It's nice to be remembered," she said during a recent interview, "but I was brought up to admire people for what they do to help others—not what they have done for themselves."

Now a widow, Mrs. Miller lives alone in the Los Feliz section of Los Angeles.

Jay Jostyn played the title role of *Mr. District Attorney* for many years on network radio. (NBC photo)

"MISTER DISTRICT ATTORNEY"

Radio's famous crime fighter was created in 1939 to fill the gap left at NBC when *Amos 'n Andy* moved to CBS. The show's producer and owner, Phillips H. Lord (living in retirement in Maine), tailored it to fit the Monday-through-Friday, 7:00-7:15 time slot vacated by its predecessor. Within a short time, however, *Mr. District Attorney* moved to Wednesday evenings, 9:30-10:00, where it remained a fixture for many years.

The first actor to essay the title role was Dwight Weist. Raymond Edward Johnson (living in Wallingford, Connecticut) replaced him, and in 1941, Jay Jostyn took over the part.

Although it was never so stated, the character of the crusading big-city D.A., who was fearless in his pursuit of crooked politicians and mobsters, was inspired by Thomas E. Dewey.[2] Before his terms as Governor of New York and the two unsuccessful presidential bids, Dewey had become nationally famous as the district attorney who ran gambling, prostitution and "Murder, Inc." out of New York City.

Mr. District Attorney, like Dewey, was decisive, dramatic and a little pompous. He was always introduced by the announcer as "Mr. District Attorney...champion of the people... defender of truth...guardian of our fundamental rights to life, liberty and the pursuit of happiness."

The program's two other running characters were the D.A.'s secretary and his trusted assistant, *Harrington*, who handled most of the really rough stuff. The latter part was played first by Walter Kinsella and then by Len Doyle. Originally the secretary was *Miss Rand*, with Arlene Francis in the role. When Vicki Vola took over the part, the name was changed to *Miss Miller*. To a regular listener with an ear for subtleties, it seemed that *Miss Miller* and her boss just might have a somewhat different and closer relationship after office hours.

Len Doyle, who played *Harrington*, posed with Jostyn and Vicki Vola, the D.A.'s secretary, *Miss Miller*.

Both *Miss Miller* and *Harrington* always called the D.A. "Chief." He also had a nickname, "Blackie," which came from his hobby of magic. His idol was supposed to be the late magician, Harry Blackstone.

The sponsor for many years was Bristol-Myers for their products—"Ipana for the smile of beauty and Sal Hepatica for the smile of health." Their commercials were heard by a buying public that kept the show among the Top Ten for all its years on the air.

Vicki Vola is still active in New York on radio and TV. Jostyn was the judge on TV's *Night Court* for its six years on the air. He lives in Hollywood.

Jostyn, who also played the father on radio's *The Parker Family*, sees many of his contemporaries at his club, The Masquers, where he lunches daily. Often there are autograph fans near its doors, requesting not only that he sign their books, but that he also recite the program's famous opening: "And it shall be my duty as District Attorney not only to prosecute to the limit of the law all persons accused of crimes perpetrated within this county but to defend with equal vigor the rights and privileges of all its citizens."

Jay Jostyn lunches almost every day at the Masquers Club in Hollywood. (Steve Webster)

Ms. Vola is divorced and lives in Manhattan. She is still active in radio and TV. (Jerald Mastroli)

In *Goodbye, Mr. Chips* (1939) Terry played four parts opposite the late Robert Donat.

TERRY KILBURN

The child actor of movies was born in London, England, on November 25, 1928.

Fascinated by Hollywood films, Terry became a local celebrity by imitating his favorite stars for passers-by on the pier at Clacton-on-Sea. A local bookmaker took him to a top theatrical agent, who almost managed to get him a screen test. When the deal fell through, he was heartsick but still very determined. His parents gambled what little money they had on their only child and brought him to Hollywood.

After a year of near starvation in Los Angeles, Kilburn got a showy part on Eddie Cantor's radio show, which, at the time, was one of the most popular on the air. MGM tested him, but he was not signed. Finally, he convinced director Sam Wood that he was right for *Lord Jeff* (1938), a Freddie Bartholomew[1] starrer.

He was then placed under contract to Metro, where he played "Tiny Tim" in *A Christmas Carol* (1938). He was also in *Sweethearts* (1938), *They Shall Have Music* (1939) and *Swiss Family Robinson* (1940) with the late Edna Best. Some of his other features were *A Yank at Eton* (1942) with Juanita "Baby Jane" Quigley (a married teacher in Berwyn, Pennsylvania), *National Velvet* (1944) and *Black Beauty* (1946).

Kilburn was one of the *Swiss Family Robinson* (1940), along with Baby Bobby Quillan, the late Thomas Mitchell and Edna Best.

Terry played "Tiny Tim" in the 1938 film *A Christmas Carol*. Reginald Owen took over the lead when Lionel Barrymore was unable to play in the picture because of an illness.

His most memorable appearance was in *Goodbye, Mr. Chips* (1939), in which he played four roles. Today, one of his closest friends is the widow of Robert Donat, who played "Chips."

Kilburn "loved every minute of it" until, at the age of 13, his studio did not pick up his option. "Suddenly, I wasn't wanted," he said in a recent interview. "I didn't understand why. It was the worst possible age to feel such a terrible rejection."

Reginald Owen, who played "Scrooge" in *A Christmas Carol*, died at the age of 85 on November 5, 1972.

He was able to work frequently on radio and in low-budget pictures, but Terry was painfully aware of his decline in status in Hollywood. He fell out of touch with the friends he had made at MGM's Little Red Schoolhouse. He watched the career of Peter Lawford, who had a small part in *Lord Jeff*, evolve into stardom.

Making it again became almost an obsession. He endured parts in "B" films such as *Bulldog Drummond at Bay* (1947), *Only the Valiant* (1951) and *Slaves of Babylon* (1953) to support himself. Every spare moment was spent acting and directing in small professional groups and on live TV. When he landed the role of "Marchbanks" in the 1952 revival of *Candida*,

Terry felt he was again on the brink of real success. Even with Olivia de Havilland in the title role, Kilburn's out-of-town notices were raves. Then, just before the play came into New York, the original director was replaced by Herman Shumlin. "Never have I experienced or even witnessed such personal abuse as he poured on me," says Kilburn. "By opening night my performance had been destroyed." After that, he took over the lead in *The Teahouse of the August Moon* when Eli Wallach left the play. His zeal for acting had, however, completely left him. "I began to realize that my drive to get bigger and better parts was ruining my life," he admitted. "In 1956, I chucked acting and devoted my energies to directing."

Terry is a bachelor and lives in Rochester, Michigan, where he is the Artistic Director of the Meadowbrook Theatre. (Michael Knowles)

Ironically, his second profession, which he has never pursued as he did acting, has won him both financial and artistic rewards. His London production of *Inherit the Wind* won him the prestigious Critics' Award. Both *Look Homeward, Angel* and *The Dark at the Top of the Stairs* made their West End bows under his direction.

He was on his way to England to play a part in the remake of *Goodbye, Mr. Chips* (1969) when he received word that his mother had suffered a stroke. Terry was unable to make the film.

Since 1970, Kilburn, who is a bachelor, and his mother have lived in Rochester, Michigan. He is the Artistic Director there of the Meadowbrook Theatre. His productions, which are all with professional casts, have lured big stars and have won for him a national reputation within his profession.

John and Corinne Calvet were married in 1948 when they were both under contract to producer Hal Wallis.

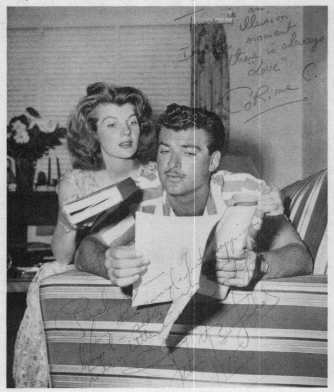

JOHN BROMFIELD

The star of "B" films who became nationally famous as the "Sheriff of Cochise" on television was born four blocks away from Notre Dame University in South Bend, Indiana. His date of birth is June 11, 1922, and his real name is Farron Bromfield. When he was two years old, his parents brought their only child to live in Venice, California.

John paid his tuition to St. Mary's College in Moraga, California, by working as a tuna fisherman during vacations. He was patching some shark gear on the pier one day when three brothers approached him about making a documentary film. The men were producers and hired him to live with Eskimos for six months in Alaska while making a movie about whaling.

Bromfield had no intention of acting again until Hal Wallis offered him a contract. The producer had seen the film *Harpoon* (1948) and signed him up for two years.

U.S. Marshal, John's second TV series, was similar to his first, *Sheriff of Cochise*.

He made *The File on Thelma Jordon* (1949), which was followed by *Paid in Full* (1950) with the late Diana Lynn, *Flat Top* (1952), *Ring of Fear* (1954) with the late Clyde Beatty and *Three Bad Sisters* (1956) with Jess Barker (working for a producer in Hollywood).

Against his agent's advice, John signed to star on TV as the "Sheriff of Cochise." He made seventy-eight half-hour episodes between 1956 and 1958 and then went right into another series, *U.S. Marshal*. As filming of the second year drew to a close, John found himself about to be divorced from his second wife, a former Goldwyn Girl named Larri Thomas. He had long before realized that he was not a dedicated actor and had begun to resent the heavy schedule his profession required. Said John recently, "When I wasn't shooting, I was signing autographs, posing for pictures or riding a horse in some damn rodeo. I had done very well financially and wanted some time for myself." At the party on the set the last day of shooting, he took his producers, Lucille Ball and Desi Arnaz, aside and told them that he was quitting the business. Both laughed. The only time he has been inside a studio since was to say hello to Lucy ten years later.

John's first wife was French sexpot Corinne Calvet.[3] They were married in 1948 when both were under contract to Hal Wallis. The couple appeared together in *Rope of Sand* (1949). After they split in 1954, he paid her alimony for four years. Recently, Corinne remarked, "When we were married, John always warned me: 'No children! No children!' The last time I saw him he was at some shopping center, surrounded by thousands of screaming kids begging for the 'Sheriff's' autograph."

Corinne Calvet today with author Richard Lamparski. She is single and living in Hollywood where she is an active member of the Arica Foundation. (David Taylor)

Bromfield and his present wife, a former Las Vegas show girl, live in a mobile-home park in Costa Mesa, California. They keep a large boat for deep-sea fishing docked nearby in the Pacific Ocean.

He spends several months a year traveling around the country with the Sportsman's Show. John is both host and co-owner of the huge attraction.

John and his wife, a former show girl, share a mobile home in Costa Mesa, California. (Zeena La Vey)

MILESTONES

1922 Born June 11, South Bend, Indiana

1948 Debuted in *Harpoon*. Signed by Hal Wallis and married Corinne Calvert

1956-58 Starred on TV in *Sheriff of Cochise*

1960 Completed his *U.S. Marshal* series and retired from show business

JETTA GOUDAL

Screenland magazine's issue of September, 1927 had Jetta Goudal on its cover.

PRICE 25 CENTS

Screenland

JETTA GOUDAL, *Drawn by*

The silent star who fought the Hollywood system and won came to the United States in 1918. In France, she had appeared in a repertory company. The exact date and place of her birth has been a mystery from the start of her career. Some sources have her being born in Versailles, France, on July 18, 1898. Another has her origin as The Hague. It has also been reported that she was born in Java, the daughter of the famed seductress Mata Hari. A few of her contemporaries maintain that she hails from New York's Lower East Side. Ms. Goudal says, "I was born on the moon, 2,000 years ago." She does not believe artists should discuss their private lives with the press.

Lupe Velez points an accusing finger at Jetta in a scene from *Lady of the Pavements* (1929). On the right is William Boyd, who had a career in talkies as "Hopalong Cassidy." The silent was directed by D.W. Griffith.

With interior decorator Harold Grieve in 1931, shortly after their marriage.

Jetta's reputation among theatregoers was made after she was seen on Broadway in *The Hero* and *The Elton Case* in 1920. Moviemakers and fans were even more impressed after they saw her in the silent *The Bright Shawl* (1923). After that picture, she signed agreements with two studios and was brought to Hollywood, where she was hailed as "a cocktail of emotions." Another of the titles given her by press agents was "the girl with the inscrutable face and expressive hands."

Although she seems as well remembered for her temperament as for her films, Ms. Goudal has always denied that she was ever difficult. But the publicity amused her and helped at the box office. Being cast again and again as the temptress only added to her public image.

Some of her 18 films were *Open All Night*

(1924), *The Spaniard* (1925) with Ricardo Cortez[2] (now a New York City stockbroker), *Three Faces East* (1926), *White Gold* (1927), *The Cardboard Lover* (1928), *Lady of the Pavements* (1929) and *Le Spectre Vert* (1930).

When Cecil B. DeMille, who had signed her to a five-year contract in 1927, did not honor the clause that gave her a raise after each six-month interval, she did what, at the time, was unthinkable. She sued. DeMille countered by accusing her of unprofessional behavior, something many people were quite willing to believe after all the stories they had read about her. The judge concerned himself only with the facts and Ms. Goudal won a settlement of $31,000. This verdict set a legal precedent that changed the producer-star relationship forever. By that ruling in 1928, it was legally established that the actor had the right to voice his or her own opinions about a part.

Having survived the suit that many had warned her would be professional suicide, Jetta then joined the handful of stars who had the courage to begin an actors' union. The studios vehemently opposed the movement and let it be known that anyone who participated in it would find himself "washed-up in Hollywood." The result was the formation of the Screen Actors Guild. The damage to the careers of the leaders, however, was incalculable.

Her last picture was a talkie, *Business and Pleasure* (1932), which starred Will Rogers. In it, her charming accent proved that she could easily have made the transition to sound films.

Instead, Jetta chose to devote her time to being the wife of Harold Grieve, a prominent interior decorator.

Ms. Goudal has been confined to a wheelchair since an accident in 1973. Said a friend recently, "She's very amusing about her situation, as she is about everything else. Her friends are the complainers. We miss her cooking, which is just about the best in Los Angeles." She is still a movie fan and her clothes are as chic as ever.

The woman whom film historian DeWitt Bodeen calls "Hollywood's *femme fatale par excellence*" has kept in touch with many of her loyal fans. Not long ago, one apologized for his handwriting. He was unsure of its legibility because he was blind. The following Christmas, his favorite star sent him an electric typewriter with a Braille keyboard.

She is seen frequently at movie functions in Hollywood. (Jon Virzi)

BRUCE BENNETT

In 1943 alone, Bruce appeared in ten feature films.

The handsome movie actor was born Herman Brix in Tacoma, Washington, on May 19, 1909. He was a star athlete at the University of Washington and distinguished himself at the intercollegiate and world competition before winning a silver medal at the 1928 Olympics in the shot-put competition.

He was still using his original name when he made *The New Adventures of Tarzan* in 1935. It was released as a feature and in serial form.

THE GREATEST TARZAN OF ALL TIME!

HERMAN BRIX

WORLD FAMOUS ATHLETE and OLYMPIC GAMES CHAMPION

in **EDGAR RICE BURROUGHS'**

THRILLING NEW PICTURE

THE *NEW ADVENTURES of*

TARZAN

with ULA HOLT FRANK BAKER LEWIS SARGENT

and a Tremendous Supporting Cast of BURROUGHS-TARZAN ENTERPRISE

CHAPTER 11. DEATH'S FIREWORKS

FILMED IN GUATEMALA BY THE ASHTON-DEARHOLT EXPEDITION

Douglas Fairbanks, Sr., and director Sam Wood both urged him to try his luck in movies. Brix's initial film effort, *Touchdown* (1931), was marred by his breaking his shoulder during the first take. MGM seriously considered him for *Tarzan*, but chose Johnny Weissmuller[1] instead. Brix did, however, play the Ape Man twice. The first, *The New Adventures of Tarzan* (1935), was released both as a feature and a serial. While filming *Tarzan and the Green Goddess* (1938), the producers went broke, and Brix was stranded in Guatemala.

He made such "B's" as *A Million to One* (1936), *Two Minutes to Play* (1937) and *Amateur Crook* (1938). Then Columbia Pictures changed his name to Bruce Bennett, but did little else for him. His new name was listed eighth in *My Son is Guilty* (1939) with Jacqueline Wells, who later became famous as Julie Bishop (married now to a Beverly Hills physician). He was a believable if unexciting Western hero in *Blazing Six Shooters* (1940), and he and the late Rochelle Hudson[3] were *The Officer and the Lady* (1941).

Bruce played the ape man again in *Tarzan and the Green Goddess* (1938).

Warner Brothers saw star potential in him; there was even talk of their putting him opposite Bette Davis in a film version of *Ethan Frome,* but it never came about. He did turn up in some important pictures, but always as the trusted friend, discarded lover or loyal husband of a star. At least they were "A's": *Mildred Pierce* (1945), *A Stolen Life* (1946), *Nora Prentiss* (1947) and *The Treasure of Sierra Madre* (1948). His own favorite is *Sahara* (1943).

He was active throughout the '50s, but no part won him a following or even much notice. A few of his later efforts were *The Great Missouri Raid* (1950), *Sudden Fear* (1952), *Strategic Air Command* (1955), *Love Me Tender* (1956) and *Flaming Frontier* (1958). Among his last were *Alligator People* (1959) and an episode on the *Lassie* TV series.

For a while, Bruce was an executive with a restaurant chain. For the past five years, he has been buying run-down property, renovating it and selling it again at a handsome profit. He is also a licensed real-estate broker. He does not, however, consider himself retired from acting.

Married to the same woman for many years, Bennett is the father of a son and a daughter. The couple live in the Palms area of West Los Angeles.

He is very frank in admitting that he wishes he had made more of a mark than he did in his over 80 feature films. Asked whether he always got along with the stars and directors with whom he worked, Bennett replied: "Yes, I think they all liked me, but I never made close friends with any of them. I don't really swing. Never did. I think I must have come across as kind of a square."

Today Bennett is a real estate man in West Los Angeles. (Michael Knowles)

Bobby Diamond
of
FURY

The late Bill Fawcett played "Bill," the foreman of "The Broken Wheel Ranch." Peter Graves was "Jim Newton," owner of the ranch and foster father of "Joey."

The story of a boy and his horse premiered on NBC-TV on Saturday morning, October 15, 1955. It remained on the network for five seasons and is still in syndication under the title, *Brave Stallion*. One hundred-fourteen 30-minute films were made, all of them in black and white.

Bobby Diamond was featured on the covers of the *Fury* comic books, which were very popular in the 1960s.

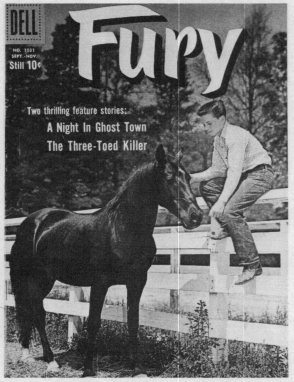

DELL

NO. 1031
SEPT.-NOV.
Still 10¢

Fury

Two thrilling feature stories:
A Night In Ghost Town
The Three-Toed Killer

Bobby Diamond, who played the lead, "Joey," had been a professional since he could walk. His mother, who had been a vocalist with Danny Thomas, did her best to get him into movies. By the time he was two years old, he had been on the covers of *Collier's* and *Parade* magazines. She had two other children, but her efforts were concentrated on Bobby. "Probably," says Bobby, "because she got such a positive response from me. I thoroughly enjoyed everything I did in front of a camera."

Diamond was born in Los Angeles on August 23, 1943. His father was in real estate.

The opening episode of the series had "Joey" fighting in the street. Someone threw a bottle, and he was taken into custody by a policeman. "Jim Newton," who was played by Peter Graves, saw the incident and assisted in his defense in court. When the judge learned that "Joey" was an orphan, he allowed "Newton" to take him to live on his ranch, "The Broken Wheel."

"Today," says Diamond, "the kids are so hip they'd size up the situation as a gay relationship. But I was twelve years old when I signed for the series. I believed as much in those plots as our viewers did. I was so square I even ate the sponsor's product (Post Toasties)."

The other running character was the older man, "Pete," who was played by William Fawcett. He died January 25, 1974. Bobby liked him and Peter Graves and everyone else connected with the show, including the star, the horse Fury.

After *Fury's* cancellation in 1960, Bobby turned down a chance to be one of Fred MacMurray's three sons on television in favor of a role on Nanette Fabray's short-lived series. After that, he had a running part on *Dobie Gillis*.

Since 1971, Diamond has been practicing law in Westwood Village, California. He specializes in criminal and personal injury cases. He still acts whenever a job is offered and in the past few years has been seen on *Banyon* and in a Johnson's Wax commercial. Recently, he explained his change of careers: "Just when I was going into my teens, my mother died. I always felt I could do whatever a part called for, but I never had to deal with agents and casting people. She had done it for me. When *Fury* was over, I found I was really on my own. I don't miss acting like I probably would in another profession because every time I face a jury it's like my big scene."

Diamond is also quite an accomplished gymnast, as he proved during a recent interview, when he stood on one hand on top of his desk.

He still sees many of the people with whom he worked. One close friend is Tommy Rettib,[4] who was the first boy to play Lassie's master on television.

Bobby, who has never married, lives alone "most of the time" in a hillside house in Studio City. Recently he disclosed his attitude toward being recognized: "Everyone who knows me is within five years of my own age. They feel they grew up with me. Can you imagine how far ahead that puts me with chicks? It's better than residuals!"

Bobby is now a criminal lawyer. The walls of his offices in Westwood, California, are covered with oils he has painted. (Richard Schaeffer)

VINCE BARNETT

The comic who became even more famous for his jokes off-screen than on was born in Pittsburgh on July 4, 1902. He debuted on stage when he was four years old, playing "Snookums" in *Bringing Up Father.*

Barnett might never have done another thing in show business if his parents hadn't gotten him a part in the *Earl Carroll Vanities* (1927). He had been piloting the Pittsburgh-Cleveland mail plane, and they were concerned for his safety. Although Vince still flies, he has been a performer ever since.

Vince was always putting someone on.

Myrna Loy and the late Max Baer enjoy their coffee break while Vince camps it up. The three were making *The Prizefighter and the Lady* (1933) when this photo was taken.

The elder Barnett was very well-known among show people for a routine he did as an insulting waiter, and his son soon picked it up. Vince, using various accents and disguises, became a put-on artist of such a reputation that he was sought out by the famous, wealthy and powerful to heckel, harass and infuriate their own kind. At various times, his outrageousness was unleashed on George Bernard Shaw, Clark Gable, Jerry Giesler, Louis B. Mayer, Winston Churchill and Al Capone. No one ever did anything but laugh when the ploy was revealed. However, George Marshall, who had borne the brunt of one of his pranks, waited a year and then quietly abandoned him in a high-security area of an air base during a tour. Barnett spent the next few hours with intelligence officers who were very unamused.

One star who found the little guy with the big, rude mouth unfunny was Paul Muni. Says Vince, "Muni was a friend, but he had no humor whatsoever." Two others whom Barnett found humorless were the late Ben Blue[4] and Marlon Brando.

He came to Hollywood in 1928 and did a few small parts in such films as *All Quiet on the Western Front* (1930). Howard Hawks saw Barnett rib the late Bobby Jones[1] and gave him a role in *Scarface* (1932). He was an immediate hit with the public. The film's producer, Howard Hughes, hired him to pull gags on people.

Throughout the '30s and '40s, he made pictures such as *Riffraff* (1935), *A Star is Born* (1937), *Seven Sinners* (1940), *The Killers* (1946), *Brute Force* (1947) and *Knock on Any Door* (1949). He was a fixture in the "Big Town" series for Paramount.

Financially, Barnett has no worries. Since he had never signed a long-term contract during his heyday, whenever his services were required in any of the 100-odd features he made, he commanded a substantial free-lance fee. From 1955 to 1961, he owned and operated a bar and grill in Santa Monica that catered to the aviation trade. He lives in Sherman Oaks, California, with a woman he married three months after the death of his first wife in 1955.

Today when Barnett is seen, it is usually on TV. He maintains that he is a victim of a left-wing blacklist. "I am a 100 per cent American patriot," he told an interviewer recently. "Today, the business of features is being run for and by the same Commie bums who were saving their skins by copping the Fifth Amendment twenty years . I haven't forgotten them, and I don't forgive them. Who would want to appear in the filth they're making today, anyway?"

His long-time close friend is Pat O'Brien.

Barnett beside some of his aviation citations. (Paul Schaeffer)

MILESTONES

1902   Born on Independence Day in Pittsburgh

1906   Debuted on stage as *Snookums*

1927   Gave up flying mail plane to appear in Earl Carroll Vanities

1930   Made his first movie, *All Quiet on the Western Front*

1932   Clicked in *Scarface*

1955-61 Ran his own bar and grill in Santa Monica

ANDREA LEEDS

The movie star of the '30s was born on August 18, 1914, in Butte, Montana.

When she graduated from UCLA it was with the intention of becoming a screenwriter. To support herself she began appearing in short subjects under her real name, Antoinette Lees. Although she was hailed as a "discovery" of Howard Hawks, Andrea had appeared in a low-budget western, *Song of the Trail* (1936) opposite the late Kermit Maynard, before she met the director.

In the late '30s, the late Samuel Goldwyn gave Andrea the full star treatment. By 1940 she had married and retired.

The late Chet Huntley interviewing Andrea at a movie premiere in the 1930s.

She made quite a splash in *Come and Get It* (1936) and was placed under contract to the late Samuel Goldwyn. She made an even stronger impression in *Stage Door* (1937). The scene in which she slowly climbs the stairs to her subsequent suicide earned her an Oscar nomination.

With such glowing reviews and the prestigious Goldwyn Studios behind her, it is both odd and regrettable that Andrea's career fizzled out so quickly. She was never again given the chance to follow up those two performances with another really strong role. In a recent interview she admitted that her heart was never really in her career.

She was very much in love with Jack Dunn, the skating partner of the late Sonja Henie.[1] He seemed slated for a movie career when he was stricken with the rare disease, tularemia. His sudden death on July 16, 1938, left her devastated.

In 1939 Andrea married the handsome young Robert S. Howard. His father, who owned the famed race horse Seabiscuit, left him over $5,000,000 when he died. For years her husband owned and operated the Howard Manor, one of the best hotels in Palm Springs.

Don Ameche and Al Jolson were her co-stars in *Swanee River* (1939).

Katherine Hepburn counsels Andrea in a scene from the film *Stage Door* (1937). Her portrayal of the girl who finally commits suicide earned her a nomination for the Best Supporting Actress of the year.

Her refined features and gentle manner disappeared from the screen after *Earthbound* (1940). True to her word, she retired after her marriage. Some of her earlier credits were: *Youth Takes a Fling* (1938) with Joel McCrea,[3] *They Shall Have Music* (1939) and *The Real Glory* (1939). In *The Goldwyn Follies* (1938), in which opera star Helen Jepson (living in Orange, New Jersey) made her only film appearance, Andrea had a duet with Kenny Baker[2] of George Gershwin's last hit song, "Love Walked In." Actually, her vocalistics were dubbed by Virginia Verrill.

Film historian Don Miller has said of Andrea Leeds: "For one so young she had remarkable technical control, assurance and poise. An especially expressive throaty voice. Had she continued in pictures, she could have performed with similar advantage the parts that went to Olivia de Havilland."

The actress who played opposite such stars as Al Jolson, David Niven and Gary Cooper does not miss Hollywood and almost never visits it. Her sole friend from those days is Shirley Mason, the silent star and sister of Viola Dana.[5]

Andrea lives all year around in a luxurious, refrigerated home that she shares with her housekeeper and two schnauzers. Her neighbor is Ruth Taylor, co-star in the original production of *Gentlemen Prefer Blondes* and the mother of screenwriter Buck Henry.

Andrea has owned and managed a fashionable jewelry shop in Palm Springs for over 20 years. (Richard Shaeffer)

Andrea was widowed in 1962. Ten years later her only daughter died. Her son lives in the mountains not far from Palm Springs. She spends every weekday at the custom jewelry shop she has owned and managed for over 20 years.

Milestones

1914   Born in Butte, Montana on August 18th

1936   Debuted in movies opposite Kermit Maynard

1936   Clicked in *Come and Get It!* and was signed by Samuel Goldwyn

1937   Nominated for an Academy Award

1938   Her fiance died suddenly

1939   Married handsome young millionaire

1940   Made her film swan song and retired

George Burns and Gracie Allen in 1938, several years after they adopted Sandra and Ronnie.

RONNIE BURNS

The young man who became nationally famous as the son of George Burns and Gracie Allen was born in Evanston, Illinois, on July 9, 1935. Orphaned, he was adopted by the famous comedy team when he was only a few months old and grew up in Beverly Hills.

Ronnie's parents never suggested he become an actor. When he attended the cinema department of U.S.C., it was to study film production. After graduating he worked for three years as an editor at the General Service Studios, where the *Burns and Allen* TV program was filmed. It was Ralph Levy, who, at the time, was directing the comedy pair, who suggested Ronnie be added to the cast. After studying acting for six weeks at the Pasadena Playhouse, he began playing himself.

Ronnie and his father continued for a full season on television after Gracie Allen retired in 1958. (National Broadcasting Company)

The show's writers had known him since he was a little boy; so, while the plots were fictitious, his character wasn't. If there was ever a line of dialogue he felt uncomfortable with, it was quickly changed. He remained with the series even after his mother retired in 1958. After it went off the air at the end of the following season, he did a few guest appearances on shows such as *Playhouse 90.* In 1960, he starred on NBC's summer replacement series, *Happy.* After that, he worked with his father's company, which produced the series *Wendy and Me* and *No Time for Sergeants.* When the latter was cancelled in 1965, he quit.

Ronnie's attitude toward his career is a curious one. He admits that being Ronnie Burns helped rather than hindered him with girls. He allowed during a recent interview that acting on television never bored him — "the pace was too quick to ever be dull." When pressed for a reason for his present total lack of interest in any phase of show business, all he could say was, "I can't put my finger on why, but I came to really dislike it."

He is now involved in buying and selling of condominiums. "I don't miss the show business one bit and nothing would tempt me to go back into it," he has said. "Anyway, what you don't enjoy you don't do very well. I was never much of an actor."

Ronnie has three sons by his wife, a non-professional. They were recently divorced. He lives by himself in Marina Del Rey, California.

His sister, Sandra, who is also adopted, seldom appeared on the series. She is married to the son of architect Charles Luckman. They live in San Diego and spent most of their time on their large boat.

Ronnie Burns has almost no friends in show business, but he has remained very close to his dad and the two have dinner together several times a week. He says he never realized just how famous and well liked his parents were until he began making personal appearances with them when he was on their show. "People always ask me if my mother was funny at home," says Ronnie. "Yes, she was funny. It was fun growing up with both of my folks. But the side of my mother the public never saw was the most wonderful one. I feel very, very lucky that they chose me to be their son."

Ronnie and his wife had three sons before they were divorced. He now lives in Marina Del Rey, California. (Michael Knowles)

Cheesecake photos of Adele were on the walls of barracks everywhere U.S. servicemen were stationed during World War II.

ADELE MARA

The movie actress and star of cheesecake photos was born Adelaida Delgado on April 28, circa 1927, in Highland Park, Michigan. Her parents, who were born in Spain, permitted her to take dancing lessons from the time she was six years old. By the time she was ten, she was charging 50 cents per child to give lessons in her basement.

Adele and her brother were barely in their teens when they debuted with Xavier Cugat for a three-week engagement at Detroit's Statler Hotel. The following summer, she took a bus to New York City and continued her dancing studies until she ran out of money. She asked Cugat for advice, and he put her into his act at the Waldorf-Astoria, where she stayed for nine months.

Movie mogul Harry Cohn saw her and signed Adele up for his Columbia Pictures. The studio had her tutored in acting by the late Josephine Hutchinson, Clark Gable's first wife.

Adele posed for this picture in the 1940's when Daylight Saving Time was still unfamiliar to Americans.

Among her last features was *The Big Circus* with Gilbert Roland and David Nelson in 1959.

The first kiss in her life came from Larry Parks during a screen test.

Adele made pictures such as *The Fighting Seabees* (1944), in which she did a jitterbug with John Wayne, and *Flame of the Barbary Coast* (1945), but it was in pin-up art that she came into her own. She posed for over 4,000 cheesecake stills that adorned barracks of U.S. installations all over the world during World War II.

Columbia dropped her after two years and she moved to Republic Pictures for a long stay. She loved making movies but never developed a great ambition for stardom. The only time she was really disappointed was when she lost the role in *The Moon and Sixpence* to Elena Verdugo because her studio refused to loan her out. She appeared in one cheapie after another: *Blackmail* (1947), *I, Jane Doe* (1948) with Vera Hruba Ralston[4] and *California Passage* (1950). Although she made two big-budget films with John Wayne, *Wake of the Red Witch* (1948) and *Sands of Iwo Jima* (1950), today when she sees him she is too shy to speak. "I doubt he'd remember me," she explained recently. The only ones she sees from her heyday are Esther Williams and her husband, Fernando Lamas.

Among her last pictures were: *Count the Hours* (1953), *Back from Eternity* (1956) and *The Big Circus* (1959).

Adele and her family of three boys live on an estate in Los Angeles with live-in servants and four thoroughbred horses. (Richard Schaeffer)

In 1953 she married a producer—"The smartest thing I ever did," says Adele. "The second smartest thing" that she says she ever did was to have three sons. Adele and her family live on a six-acre estate in a canyon in West Los Angeles, complete with live-in servants, her parents, four thoroughbred horses and twelve beehives. She is a liberal Democrat, a tireless worker for the John Tracy Clinic and a superb cook.

Adele Mara lost interest in acting after her marriage, although she appeared on several *Maverick* episodes that her husband produced. Recently he used Adele for some dubbing. When her job was finished, she began drawing unemployment compensation, which she uses to buy her favorite luxury—fresh Iranian caviar.

"Flicka" was a four-year-old Arabian sorrel mare whose real name was "Wahama."

JOHN WASHBROOK

"Flicka's" friend was born in Toronto, Canada, on October 16, 1944. His parents encouraged the acting ambitions of John and his older brother. Both appeared frequently on a local children's radio program.

When he was ten years old, his mother brought him to New York City during the Easter school vacation. They stayed with an actress who was a family friend. John went off with her on an interview and was picked for the lead role on the prestigious *U.S. Steel Hour.*

Almost immediately he got two other major TV shows and was signed by Twentieth Century-Fox for their first television series, *My Friend Flicka.*

Flicka had been a big hit as a feature in 1943. To insure its success as a series, production chief Buddy Adler allowed a large budget and assigned a crew that included some of the best technicians on the lot. It was photographed in color, which was somewhat unusual in 1955. Another Adler touch was to cast his wife, Anita Louise, in the part of John's mother.

Washbrook has high praise for everything and everyone connected with the series with the exception of the late Miss Louise. He found her "cold" and says that she kept the cast and crew waiting repeatedly.

He played "Ken McLaughlin," who lived in Wyoming on the "Goose Bar Ranch." Gene Evans took the part of his father. "Flicka" was a four-year-old Arabian sorrel mare whose real name was "Wahama." John's stand-in .was a girl who was an expert rider.

Although *Flicka* was a hit, its high overhead made it economically impractical to continue production. After 39 weeks on the CBS network in 1956, it was cancelled. Since then, the half-hour segments have been shown on NBC, ABC and again on CBS. *Flicka* is still in syndication.

Gene Evans and the late Anita Louise played Johnny's parents on the series.

When filming ceased, she was sold to a wealthy New Mexico man, who gave her to his daughter.

When John signed for the series he had never seen the movie nor had he ever read the Mary O'Hara book. He immediately began riding lessons, although when he reported for rehearsals he found that he had learned to ride English saddle instead of the Western style that was required.

He speaks with great affection of "Flicka" and would like to know whether she is still alive.

On the strength of his *Flicka* popularity, Washbrook toured with rodeos and starred in the DuPont TV special, *The Prince and the Pauper*. He lost the part of Deborah Kerr's son in *The King and I* because it was being filmed at the same time as his series. After *Flicka,* he had roles in *The Space Children* (1958) and *Lonelyhearts* (1959).

Since 1970, John has been living in a brownstone on the West Side of Manhattan with a young woman named Joy. He still hears from Bobby Diamond, his competitor on *Fury,* and he is a friend of Roddy McDowall, who played the part of the boy in the original *Flicka* movie. He works steadily, acting in off-Broadway plays, repertory companies and dinner theatres on the East Coast.

Johnny and a young woman share an apartment in a brownstone in Manhattan.

He is recognized frequently by people of his own age group and enjoys talking with them about the show. The only disadvantage he has found is that many fans and fellow actors assume that he is well-off from his days as a network television star. "It's true that my parents put all the money I made in the bank for me," he explained recently. "But when my older brother quit acting and asked me to go into business with him, I declined. Instead, I invested all my savings. He went bankrupt." Asked whether the loss bothered him, he replied, "No, because it gave me a chance to decide whether I really wanted to continue acting. It also has brought my brother and me even closer."

Phyllis in 1941 posed with the late Erich Von Stroheim, who was publicized during his career as "The Man You Love to Hate."

PHYLLIS BROOKS

The lovely blonde of stage and screen was born Phyllis Seiler in Boise, Idaho, on July 18, 1914. Her father, an industrial engineer, moved his family from St. Paul to Milwaukee and finally to New York City.

When the Seilers began to feel the effects of the Great Depression, Phyllis began modeling to help out. One of her first jobs was for Ipana Toothpaste. After someone at Universal Pictures saw her in the advertisement, she was tested and given a stock contract. She lasted a year there and then moved to RKO.

Among her early pictures were *I've Been Around* (1934) and *McFadden's Flats* (1935), with Betty Furness and the late Richard Cromwell.

When Phyllis was dropped by RKO, she went to New York and landed a part in the original cast of *Stage Door* (1936). It was from that smash hit that she was signed to a much better contract by Twentieth Century-Fox. When the play was filmed by RKO, the part she had played went to Ginger Rogers. Phyllis also did *Panama Hattie* (1940) on Broadway.

She feels her versatility worked against her. "I was always the second choice," she said recently. "I got very weary of substituting for others." The late Josef von Sternberg borrowed her for his picture *The Shanghai Gesture* (1941) and then subjected her to great personal abuse. After a week of this treatment, she refused to return to the set. Says Phyllis, "From that moment on, he couldn't have been nicer to me."

Phyllis and George Murphy supported Shirley Temple in *Little Miss Broadway* (1938). The former U.S. Senator is now in public relations in Los Angeles.

Another 20th Century-Fox contract player, Gene Tierney, shares a laugh with Phyllis at the Mocombo.

Director Josef von Sternberg borrowed her for *The Shanghai Gesture* (1941) and then subjected her to personal abuse on the set. This photo was taken shortly before he died on December 22, 1969.

The part Phyllis played in *Stage Door* on Broadway went to Ginger Rogers when the play was filmed.

Phyllis appeared in *City Girl* (1937) with Ricardo Cortez. She also graced two "Charlie Chan" features and two Shirley Temple vehicles and was in *Slightly Honorable* (1940) with the late Claire Dodd, *Lady in the Dark* (1944) and *The Unseen* (1945) with the late Gail Russell.

During World War II, Phyllis made a 23,000-mile tour of the South Pacific for the USO. Then, a few days before V-J Day in 1945, she married a young man whom Louella Parsons described in her column as "a very rich socialite." He was also the former Harvard roommate of John F. Kennedy. The late President was the godfather to their first son.

In the early '50s she was the host of an afternoon movie on a Boston TV station. Her main interests these days are her family of four children, oil painting and cooking.

Phyllis summers in Ogunquit, Maine. The rest of the year she lives in Washington, D.C., and Malden, Massachusetts. Her husband, Torbert H. MacDonald, has been the Democratic Congressman from Massachusetts' Seventh District since 1954. Until they married, his wife had been a registered Republican.

Today she is married to a Congressman from Malden, Massachusetts. Her oldest son is the godchild of President John F. Kennedy. (Jeanne Youngson)

Warner Brothers was publicizing Lyle Talbot as the handsome young bachelor in 1935.

To Alice Mae / With my best / Lyle Talbot

LYLE TALBOT

The durable movie actor was born on February 8, 1904, in Pittsburgh. As a child he toured the Midwest in tent shows. After his parents died his grandmother adopted him and changed his last name, Henderson, to hers, which was Hollywood. He spent several years in her rooming house in Wahoo, Nebraska. One of her roomers, a sometime vaudevillian, taught Lyle magic tricks and hypnosis.

Mary Astor[4], Joyce Compton, and the late Nat Pendleton were with Lyle in *Trapped by Television*, a feature made in 1936.

After having spent six years of his teens as the juvenile lead in a Toby show and a stock company, Talbot came to New York City and made a short, *The Nightingale* (1931), with Pat O'Brien.

A Warner Brothers talent scout had seen Talbot in a play in Dallas and put him under contract. His debut was in *Love is a Racket* (1932). Lyle made a few important pictures: *20,000 Years in Sing Sing* (1933) and *Oil for the Lamps of China* (1935) with Josephine Hutchinson (married to actor Staats Cotsworth) and then began a string of "B's" so long that he is one of the leading contenders for the title "King of the Cheapies." Although he was a thoroughly competent actor, Talbot never showed much sex appeal and lacked the strong celluloid personality that could have made him a star. A sampling of his hundreds of low-budget efforts: *Trapped by Television* (1936), *Gun Town* (1937), *Change of Heart* (1938), *They Asked for It* (1939) with Tom Beck (now a realtor in Redding, Connecticut), *Parole Fixer* (1940) with William Henry (a landscape architect in the San Fernando Valley), *They Raid by Night* (1942) with Victor Varconi (living in Santa Barbara), *Strange Impersonation* (1946), *Appointment with Murder* (1948) and *Wild Weed* (1949) with Alan Baxter (living in Los Angeles). His pomaded pompadour was more often than not covered by a hat in roles as cops, reporters and gangsters.

Joyce Compton who specialized in playing dumb blondes is single and lives in Sherman Oaks, California. Her hobby is painting. (Muriel Shopwin)

He spent much of the 1950's playing the next door neighbor to Ozzie and Harriet on TV and had another running part on the *Bob Cummings Show*. He toured with Penny Singleton in *Never Too Late* in 1964 and three years later was in the New York City Center's *South Pacific*. Talbot still is active in stock and does an occasional TV shot. Among his last movies were *With a Song in My Heart* (1952), *The Great Man* (1957), *Sunrise at Campobello* (1960) and *Adventures of Batman and Robin* (1967).

Lyle has an amazing recall of his long career. He helped establish the Screen Actors Guild at a time when it was dangerous to even mention unionizing performers in Hollywood.

He and his fourth wife have been married for over twenty years. He has two sons and a daughter. The Talbots live in Studio City, California, only a few miles from his old friend Ralph Bellamy.

Lyle outside his home in Studio City, California. (Richard Schaeffer)

By 1921 Eva (left) and Jane Novak were well established as leading ladies in silent pictures.

JANE AND EVA NOVAK

The stars of silent pictures are from St. Louis, Missouri. Jane was born on January 12, 1896, and Eva on Valentine's Day, 1898.

The sisters had an aunt, Ann Schaefer, who was a player at Vitagraph. She had mentioned in a letter that the head of the studio had admired Jane's photo which was in her dressing room. Jane was on the next train to Hollywood and got a part in a picture the day she arrived. Two of her first friends were Bebe Daniels' mother and the star Ruth Roland. Both helped and encouraged her.

Jane was William S. Hart's leading lady in five of his films. For a while she was engaged to the western hero.

Hal Roach put her under contract at $10 a day. When his young comic protested that she was making more than he was, Roach worked out a percentage deal with him that was soon to make him a millionaire. His name was Harold Lloyd.

The Novaks' father had died when they were small children, and their only brother was in poor health. Mrs. Novak and her children joined Jane in 1918. Soon Eva, too, was acting in movies.

While the fact that they were sisters was featured in their publicity, the only film they ever appeared in together was *The Man Life Passed By* (1923). Jane was seen in *String Beans* (1918), *Behind the Door* (1920), *Divorce* (1923), *Closed Gates* (1927) and *Redskin* (1919 with Richard Dix. Eva made *O'Malley of the Mounted* (1921), *The Tiger's Claw* (1923), *Sally* (1925), *Irene* (1926) with George K. Arthur (living in Manhattan), *Red Signals* (1927) and *For the Term of His Natural Life* (1929).

Jane with William S. Hart who is holding Mary Jane Irving. The three played in *Square Deal Man* (1917).

The sisters were expecially popular as leading ladies to Western stars. Eva was in ten pictures opposite Tom Mix. Jane was with William S. Hart in five of his features and, for a while, they were engaged. Although they didn't marry, he is considered the big love of her life. She still visits his ranch in Newhall, California, which is open to the public as a museum.

Sound all but ended Jane's career. Her appearances in talkies were few and brief: *Hollywood Boulevard* (1936), *Foreign Correspondent* (1940), *Desert Fury* (1947). Eva, however, worked on for over twenty years as a bit player and extra.

Jane dated Donald Crisp in her youth. They were still friends when he died on May 25, 1974.

Mary Jane Irving lives in Bel-Air with her husband Robert Carson, the original author of *A Star is Born*.

Jane Novak resides in Sherman Oaks with her daughter and son-in-law who is a movie producer.

Eva lives within walking distance of her sister. She has three greatgrandchildren. (Jon Virzi)

Jane lives in Sherman Oaks, California, within walking distance of Eva. They see each other often but have lost touch with almost everyone else from their era. Jane shares a house with her daughter and son-in-law Walter Seltzer, who produced *Skyjacked* and *Soylent Green.* In 1974, her cookbook *Treasury of Chicken Cookery,* was published.

One of Eva's two daughters married Jane Russell's brother. Unlike her sister, she does not look back on her heyday as a glamourous period in her life. "It was only a means to an end," she said recently. Contrary to most film buffs' recollections, she feels that Jane was a much bigger star. She recently told an interviewer, "People constantly ask me if I'm the famous Jane Novak. I feel like saying, 'Why, no. My first name is Kim!'"

EDWARD NORRIS

The actor who ruined his own career was born in Philadelphia on March 10, 1911. His father was a socially prominent doctor.

After graduating from the Culver Academy, Edward and his mother took a vacation in Coronado, California, where William Wellman was directing *Wings* (1927). After doubling for Buddy Rogers in one scene, Norris was hooked on acting. On Wellman's advice, he returned east to get some experience in a stock company.

Norris made 127 movies during his career. He specialized in playing sharp, young gangsters.

By 1932 he was back in Hollywood, acting in a little theatre production. A Russian ballerina he was living with introduced him to the director Rouben Mamoulian.

Mamoulian placed him under personal contract. After being coached by the late Akim Tamiroff, Norris was signed by MGM at a starting salary of $35 a week. His debut was with Greta Garbo and John Gilbert in *Queen Christina* (1933).

During the following six years at the studio, he made almost an many mistakes as he made pictures.

After proving himself as an actor in bits and shorts, the studio began loaning him out at handsome fees. After getting excellent notices for his lead roles in *Show Them No Mercy* (1935) and *They Won't Forget* (1937), he would return to his home lot only to be assigned walk-ons. The few times he was set for good parts in important pictures, he was replaced at the last minute by bigger names. Again and again, Norris was put on suspension while actors such as Robert Taylor, who was considered "cooperative," were being turned into stars.

His private life began to suffer as well. In 1938, the late Ann Sheridan walked out on their two-year marriage. Norris, who keeps a photo of her on his dresser, explained recently: "Annie was terrific. I don't know how she stood me that long. I was trying to drown my disappointments with alcohol."

After Metro, he went to 20th Century-Fox,

where he stayed until becoming an Air Corps instructor at the outbreak of World War II. *Tail Spin* (1939), opposite Alice Faye, was supposed to be his big chance, but it did poorly at the box office.

After the War, he signed with Universal, but his contract was torn up almost immediately due to a misunderstanding. "For once I was in the right," says Norris, "but I was too hot-headed to explain myself properly."

After the production of "B" features all but ended in the early 1950's, Edward's offers of jobs dwindled to almost nothing.

He supported Jean Parkers and the late Chester Morris in *I Live on Danger* (1942).

He was married for two years to the late Ann Sheridan in the late 1930's. He still keeps a photo of her on his dresser. (U.P.I.)

Of the 127 features he made, the most memorable are *Bad Guy* (1937), *Boys Town* (1938), *Frontier Marshal* (1939), *The Lady in Question* (1940), *Dr. Ehrlich's Magic Bullet* (1940), *The Mystery of Marie Roget* (1942), *Murder in the Music Hall* (1946) and *I Was a Communist for the F.B.I.* (1951).

Norris has some consolation in his reputation as a ladies' man. Among his female contemporaries, he is remembered quite fondly on a very personal basis. At age sixteen, he married a girl older than himself who is the mother of his only child. His second wife was Lona Andre, the runner-up in the "Panther Woman" contest. Another of his five wives was Sheila Ryan who died in 1975.

His other revenge on Hollywood is his lifestyle. He spends part of each year in one of the several properties he owns in La Paz, Mexico. Another few months, he lives on a 1,000-acre ranch near the Canadian border, where he raises cattle. The garages of his third home, which is on the ocean in Malibu, contain a Rolls-Royce, two Mercedes-Benzes, a Cadillac, a camper and a motorcycle.

Ed has a home in La Paz, one on the ocean in Malibu and a ranch near the Canadian border. (Alice Barr)

His constant companion is an Irish setter. The only connection he has with Hollywood is a friendship of many years with Patric Knowles.

Norris is over the bitterness he felt about his career: "I've lived long enough," he says, "to see that most of what happened was my own fault. I had the wrong agent, the wrong advice and the wrong attitude."

TRANSITIONS

1911	Born in Philadelphia on March 10
1927	Made screen debut in *Wings* as a double
1932	Made acting debut in *Queen Christina*
1938	Wife, Ann Sheridan, leaves him
1941	Entered Air Corps
1950's	Film career petered out

Joan's 1951 feature *On the Loose* was scripted by her parents.

JOAN EVANS

"Sam Goldwyn's Folly" was born on July 18, 1934, in New York City to Katherine Albert and Dale Eunson, both successful writers. Her parents encouraged her desire to perform. Among her earliest recollections is that she "loved to show off." She was named for Joan Crawford, who is also her godmother.

By the time she was nine years old, Joan was appearing in stock in *Guest in the House*, which her father co-authored. A family friend suggested to the talent scout for Goldwyn Studios that he consider her. She was signed to a long-term contract that began at $150.00 a week.

Her mother and father named their only child after their close friend, Joan Crawford, who is also her godmother.

Joan was schooled, groomed and highly publicized. The studio saw her as the typical teen-age girl of the period. Fan magazines agreed and gave her a great deal of space. Her life-style, which was the most distinctive thing about her, was a great help. Her parents were "modern" and gave their only child her own apartment. Readers were titillated by their permissiveness when Joan announced that she not only dyed her hair and wore low-cut dresses by also actually went out on dates unchaperoned.

Goldwyn launched her with Farley Granger in *Roseanna McCoy* (1949). She ended a 8-week publicity tour by her appearance at its New York premiere where she fainted. Audiences merely dozed off.

She was the late Audie Murphy's leading lady in *No Name on the Bullet* (1958).

Again she was with Granger (living with a friend in Rome) in *Our Very Own* (1950) and *Edge of Doom* (1950). She wasn't really bad in her films, but neither was she good enough to live up to the expectations the studio's publicity generated, nor was she able to create a real following. Still Goldwyn continued the star treatment for five years.

Among her dozen features were *Skirts Ahoy!* (1952) with Keefe Brasselle (a Beverly Hills businessman), *On the Loose* (1951) with Robert Arthur (who runs a little theatre group in Los

Angeles), *The Outcast* (1954), *The Flying Fontaines* (1959) and her last, *The Walking Target* (1960).

Shortly after her career was launched, Joan met Kirby Weatherly at a diction class and announced he was to be her "protege." They eloped with Joan Crawford's aid and encouragement in 1952. By then, he had decided against acting and is now an automobile salesman.

Joan in a publicity shot with the then unknown Hugh O'Brien.

The last acting Joan did was in 1961 on *The Tall Men* on TV. She says at first she missed the profession very much but became concerned about her two children. "I thought that I would hate myself if I found out too late that I had not been with them enough," she admitted recently.

Joan Evans is now a partner in the Carden Academy in Van Nuys, California. She has no teaching degree, but California does not require one in private schools.

Joan is now the co-owner of a private elementary school in Van Nuys, California. (Linda Cury)

Her one regret concerning Hollywood is that Goldwyn refused to loan her out for *A Place in the Sun*. It may have been the turning point in her curious career. The part went instead to Shelley Winters, who was nominated for an Oscar as Best Actress of 1951 for her work in the film and who established herself as a serious actress with the role.

HIGHLIGHTS

1934—Born on July 18th in New York City.

1943—Debuts in summer stock.

1949—Starred in film *Roseanna McCoy*.

1950—Goldwyn refuses to loan her out for *A Place in the Sun*.

1952—Elopes with the help of Joan Crawford.

1961—Retires from acting.

Catcher Roy Campanella, outfielder Larry Doby, Don Newcombe and the late Jackie Robinson made baseball history when they became the first blacks to play in an All-Star Game. The date was July 12, 1949.

DON NEWCOMBE

One of the first black baseball players to break into the major leagues was born in Madison, New Jersey, on June 14, 1926. He was nine years old when he first took batting practice with a semiprofessional club managed by his older. brother.

In the spring of 1944, Don joined the New Jersey Eagles of the Negro League, winning seven games that season and losing five. Pitching for his league in the All-Star Game of 1945, Newcombe held a team of white major league opponents hitless for three innings until he developed a sore elbow. From this game, he was signed by the Dodgers. Originally, it was to play for their "Brown Dodgers," which was to be a team in the proposed new U.S. Negro League. However, after the late Jackie Robinson broke down the barrier against blacks playing major league baseball, Don was sent to the Dodgers' Class B New England League. His battery mate was Roy Campanella. The two worked closely, developing Newcombe's control of the curve.

Only when the Dodgers' pitching virtually collapsed in May of 1949 was Don allowed to join his parent team, although he had done extremely well with their New England and Montreal clubs.

In that first season he registered five shutouts, had a 7-8 season and beat every other National League team at least once. He went 32 consecutive innings without yielding a run. During the All-Star Game, Don pitched two and one-third innings for the National League. Even though he lost the first and fourth World Series games that year, Newcombe was the overwhelming choice in the polls of the Baseball Writers Association and the *Sporting News* as 1949's Rookie of the Year.

The next season he played in forty games, winning nineteen and losing eleven. In 1951, he won twenty games and lost eight, leading the National League in strikeouts (164).

Returning from the Army in 1954, he started off poorly and was suspended briefly for insubordination. But by September of 1955, he had won ten straight. When he made the National League All-Star team, he stood 14-1. Don ended the regular season with the best pitching record in his league.

For the 1956 season his salary was $25,000. At the end of the regular playing year, he had a pitching record of twenty-seven victories and seven losses. The Baseball Writers Association picked him for Most Valuable Player in the National League. He took the Cy Young Award the same year.

The following season he was able to get a raise to $37,500. At that time, this was the most the Dodgers had ever paid a pitcher.

Roy Campanella (left) congratulates Newcombe who had just pitched his third successive shutout of the 1949 season. Don and Campanella are still good friends. (World Wide Photo)

In June of 1958, he went with the Cincinnati Reds in a swap for two of their players. The Cleveland Indians took him in trade in 1960, but they released him at the end of the season. Don then asked the Dodgers for a chance to make their team in 1961 and wound up in their farm club. His last season was in 1962, during which time he played in Japan.

By this time, Newcombe had been divorced. Then there was a declaration of bankruptcy. But it was not until 1966 that he finally faced up to his addictions to alcohol and gambling. When his second wife threatened to leave him, he swore on the head of his oldest son that he would never place another bet or take another drink. He never has.

Don lives with his second wife, two sons and a daughter in a luxury home in Woodland Hills, California. (Michael Knowles)

The athlete who was once considered to be one of the foremost speedball artists since Dizzy Dean and one of the best "hitting pitchers" of his day lives in a modern, luxury home in Woodland Hills, California. He has his own public relations firm and is the vice-president of a black-owned savings and loan company.

Drinking, says Don, made him loud and obnoxious. Sober, he is frank and specific about the unrelenting competition that lead him deeper and deeper into alcoholism. "No matter how much I drank," says Newcombe, "I was never warned by the team's management. All they ever cared about was winning. I felt that pressure to win from my early games when I played sandlot ball. And before that I had it from my dad."

Two years ago, his oldest boy quit Little League because of the obsession his team's manager had with winning. "I doubt he'll ever do anything that will make me prouder of him than I was that day," Newcombe told an interviewer recently. "He felt the fun going out of his game and he had the guts to walk away. I've raised my kids to realize more out of their sports or their jobs than getting the highest score or the biggest paycheck."

TRANSITIONS

1926	Born on June 14 in Madison, New Jersey.
1944	Joined the New Jersey Eagles.
1949	Became a Brooklyn Dodger. Named Rookie of the Year.
1951	Led National League in strike-outs.
1955	Had best pitching record in National League.
1956	Named National League's Most Valuable Player. Won Cy Young Award.
1958	Traded to Cincinnati Reds.
1962	Played his last season in Japan.
1966	Swore off gambling and alcohol.

Cobina, Jr. was signed to a contract by 20th Century-Fox in 1940.

COBINA WRIGHT, JR.

The debutante once described by her mother as " 'The Most Girl of 1939' — most publicized, most photographed, most sought after," was born Cobina Caroline Wright, Jr., in New York City on August 14, 1921.

Her only competition in 1939 was Brenda Frazier, who was also her close friend from their days at Miss Hewitt's School. They differed in their coloring — Brenda was dark and gorgeous, Cobina, Jr., was blonde and luscious — and in their money. Brenda had oodles, and the Wrights had almost none.

When she was a baby, her father, a partner in a brokerage firm, left her mother. Cobina, Sr., began arranging parties and balls among New York society for fees. A woman of legendary energy and personality, Cobina, Sr., by the 1940's had her own radio program and a widely read Hearst newspaper column.

Although Jr. had no real interest in a public life, her mother arranged for her to model for John Robert Powers. Not only did she make the covers of LIFE and *Ladies' Home Journal*, but she also became the first model to be used regularly by both *Vogue* and *Harper's Bazaar*. During the craze of society girls singing in night clubs, Cobina, Jr., led the pack, performing in the smartest clubs with more publicity than all the other debs combined. A few years after her coming out, she was on the Best-Dressed List, an honor usually reserved for older women.

When her mother moved to California, Cobina, Jr., went too and was soon signed to a 20th Century-Fox contract. Although she never amounted to very much in movies, she made a few big pictures: *Moon Over Miami* (1941), *Week-end in Havana* (1941), *Footlight Serenade* (1942) and *Something to Shout About* (1943). She had done quite a bit of summer stock and was in one Broadway play, *Lorelei* (1938).

One thing her mother didn't arrange was her marriage in 1941 to Palmer Beaudette. The two disliked each other from the day they met until Sr. died in 1970 at the age of 83. The following year, Cobina's husband died, and she learned that the enormous income from his trust fund would end immediately.

Although she still lives well in a brand new home overlooking the San Ysidro Valley, it is a modest life-style compared with the lavish one she once had. One of her neighbors in Solvang is Kenny Baker,[3] whom she has never met. She refers to herself as a "reformed alcoholic."

The irrepressible Cobina Wright gives her daughter a kiss of encouragement. It was her mother who named her "the MOST girl of 1939."

Cobina is adamant in her refusal to discuss her romance in the late '30's with Price Philip. His photo, as well as one of Robert Stack, adorns her bedroom. Her only contact with Brenda Frazier over the last thirty years has been the Christmas cards they exchange.

Her three oldest children, boys, have married, and Cobina is now a grandmother. She speaks of her mother with detached amusement and denies that they are anything alike. When asked to pose for a photo, however, she insisted her 16-year-old daughter also be in it. Cee Cee, whose real name is Cobina Wright, III, wants to be an actress and model.

Cobina Wright III and Cobina, Jr. in their home in Solvang, California. (Shelly Davis)

Calleia was named "The Maltese Menace" by studio publicists.

JOSEPH CALLEIA

"The Maltese Menace" was born on August 4, 1897. His father, an architect, allowed him to study voice in preparation for an operatic career. He debuted as a chorus boy in *Cavalleria Rusticana* at the Royal Opera House in Malta.

Calleia toured the Continent in concert as a tenor. In London, he appeared in several musicals and in vaudeville.

New York first saw him in 1918 doing an imitation of the famous Scottish entertainer, Sir Harry Lauder. He was soundly panned. Briefly, he was Eduardo Ciannelli's understudy in *Have a Heart* (1918) on Broadway. Between stage engagements, he worked as a trunk repairer, piano salesman and assistant stage manager. In *The Broken Wing* (1920), Joseph sang the song, "Adelaide," which he co-authored with George Abbott.

By 1925, he had managed to have himself presented in concert at Town Hall. The reviews were excellent, but the house was nearly empty. From then on, he concentrated on acting. On Broadway, he was seen in *Broadway* (1926), *The Front Page* (1928), *The Last Mile* (1930) and *Grand Hotel* (1930).

Joseph's swarthy looks were especially effective in *Algiers* (1938).

A very young Jackie Cooper pleads with Calleia in a scene from *Tough Guy* (1936).

Calleia's screen debut was in *His Woman* (1931). Although he played many gangsters, he was too fine an actor and too intelligent to permit himself to be typecast. In *Public Hero Number One* (1935), he had the title role, a character closely patterned after Dillinger. He played a "patent leather heavy" many times, as in *Riffraff* (1936) and *My Little Chickadee* (1940). But each of his performances was unique.

Wallace Beery had him as his Mexican sidekick in *Bad Man of Brimstone* (1938). In *The Cross of Lorraine* (1943), he was a Chilean idealist. He was the Spanish mountain chieftain in *For Whom the Bell Tolls* (1943). His only top - billed role came in *Man of the People* (1937); he played a politician.

His other screen credits include: *Marie Antoinette* (1938), *Gilda* (1946), and *Wild is the Wind* (1958).

He was the co-author of the screenplay of *Robin Hood of El Dorado* (1936).

On the set of *I Spy* in 1966, he suffered a stroke. Three years later, his wife of almost forty years died. They had no children.

Calleia returned to his native Malta, where he lived out the remaining years of his life. He composed and worked in his garden until his death in 1975.

Not long ago, he explained his attitude toward his movie career: "I spent two years under decided to free-lance. It was a choice I grow happier with all the time. I saw so many of my contemporaries—splendid artists—destroyed by absurd casting. I never looked for big parts. I wanted characters with depth. Thank God, I never had to accept a role I did not feel comfortable in."

The honesty of his performances is all the more apparent as the style of many of the stars he supported begins to date.

Joseph Calleia retired to his birthplace, Malta. He died in 1975. (Peter Schaeffer)

When Charlotte won the coveted title role in Paramount's lavish production of *Alice in Wonderland* (1933) it was thought to be her big break. Instead it turned out to be a jinx on her career in movies.

CHARLOTTE HENRY

The actress for whom Hollywood's "big break" turned out so badly was born in Brooklyn on March 3. Always fascinated by the theatre, Charlotte was chided by her family when, at a very early age, she began modeling. They were astonished when she was cast in an important role in *Courage,* a Broadway hit of 1928.

In 1929, Charlotte's mother brought her only child to Hollywood. She repeated her part in the movie version of *Courage* (1930) and enrolled at Lawlor's, the school for professional children. Some of her classmates were Frankie Darro4, the late Anita Louise and Betty Grable.

Junior Durkin, who had worked with her in *Courage*, suggested Charlotte for a play he was appearing in at the Pasadena Playhouse. By then, she had appeared in *Huckleberry Finn* (1931) and *Lena Rivers* (1932), but she was still only another featured player with limited experience.

Paramount Pictures had been conducting a highly touted "talent search" for the girl who would play the title role in *Alice in Wonderland*. Ida Lupino had been brought from England for the role but had been found unsuitable. It seemed like the part of the year for any young actress. Over 6,800 were auditioned. Thousands more from all over the world wrote to the studio, enclosing their photos and begging for a chance to be in the film.

A Paramount talent scout saw Charlotte in the play and arranged a screen test on a Monday morning. One-week-to-the-day later, Charlotte Henry began filming the high-budget classic. The studio's press department made much of her uncanny resemblance to the character as it appeared in the original Tenniel drawings. An anxious movie-going public awaited the costly feature. A new young star was expected to emerge.

The picture was released in 1933 and garnered almost unanimous praise for

Charlotte. The huge cast list was impressive but, in most cases, their make-up was such that only the keenest of buffs could recognize W. C. Fields ("Humpty-Dumpty"), Jack Oakie ("Tweedledum"), Cary Grant ("The Mock Turtle") or Gary Cooper ("The White Knight"). It did poorly at the box office.

Paramount loaned their young star out to play "Bo-Peep" in the Laurel and Hardy feature, *Babes in Toyland* (1934), and for the George Arliss starrer, *The Last Gentleman* (1934), and then released her. Through no fault of her own, she had had the misfortune of appearing in an expensive failure. Major studios wanted no part of her.

Today she is probably best known for her role of "Bo-Peep" in the 1934 picture *Babes in Toyland*. The Laurel and Hardy classic is shown in most cities on television every Christmas.

The effect of *Alice* on Charlotte's life was more than the usual story of an actress ruined by a negative association. She was also typecast, but in a most peculiar way. In a recent interview, Charlotte disclosed that from the very first week of shooting, she became aware that others around her had simply lost sight of her as a person. "I no longer existed as Charlotte Henry," she said. "With that costume, I was transformed in their minds to the creature they had read about as children. My identity was gone."

Charlotte lives alone in San Diego. Her only friend from her days in Hollywood is the silent star Baby Peggy. (Marjorie Eleanor Keyes)

She was seen in low-budget films such as *Forbidden Heaven* (1935), *The Hoosier Schoolmaster* (1935), *God's Country and the Man* (1937). Finally, she was reduced to an East Side Kids vehicle, *Bowery Blitzkrieg* (1941). In her own words: "I simply lost interest."

Charlotte and her mother ran an employment agency for a while. Then she was personal secretary for fifteen years to the Roman Catholic Bishop of San Diego. After his death, she cared for her mother until she passed away in 1971. Her one brief marriage in 1947 was unsuccessful. She now lives alone.

Recently, she spent eighteen months on the grand jury. When *Alice* was shown on TV, the other jurors began asking her the inevitable questions. Said Charlotte with a sigh of resignation: " 'Alice' reaches out and shadows my existence, even today."

Lee starred in all 164 of the half hour Adventures of *Rin Tin Tin* television shows.

LEE AAKER
OF
RIN TIN TIN

The boy who played Rin Tin Tin's master on television was born in Los Angeles on September 25, 1943. His mother, who owns a dancing studio, coached him, but it was his grandparents who really encouraged him the most. They drove the boy all over Hollywood for interviews with casting directors and agents. he debuted on a local TV show, *Fantastic Studios*, along with another unknown, Richard Beymer.[4]

Lee was picked for the lead in *The Adventures of Rin Tin Tin* by the show's producer, Herbert Leonard, who had seen his two appearances, both with Ronald Reagan, on the *Ford Theatre*. His series was first seen over the ABC Network on October 18, 1954, and lasted for four seasons. Then it was re-run over ABC and CBS until 1964. After that, it went into syndication all over the world.

He shared honors with two German shepherds. The title role was taken by the fourth-generation offspring of the original Rin Tin Tin, that had been a major attraction in silent movies. Another member of the same litter did all the stunt work. An important fringe benefit of the part was his co-star's puppy, which he received as a gift.

Lee played "Rusty B Company," a boy whose parents had been killed by Indians. He was adopted by an Army unit at Fort Apache headed by "Lt. Rip Masters," who was played by Jim L. Brown (now an executive with a large cosmetics firm). Another regular on the program was "Sgt. O'Hara," portrayed by Joe Sawyer (retired to a ranch in Oregon).

The films were shot at the movie ranch of Ray "Crash" Corrigan (living in Harbor, Oregon), the star of 1930's serials.

Lee always attended public school but was never subjected to the teasing that most child stars have to face. He knew he was famous, but the only time it seemed an advantage was when he got to meet his idol, baseball star Don Larsen (now a salesman for a paper company in San Jose, California), who was introduced to him by Mickey Mantle. He became acutely aware of his fame only when it began to fade. "Suddenly," said Aaker recently, "after the series was cancelled and I began doing guest shots, I realized that something had changed—I wasn't the center of attention any more. My folks had always told me that my career might not last, but when it happened, it was still a hard thing for me to adjust to."

Lee made a number of features such as *No Room For the Groom* (1952) with Piper Laurie (married and living in Manhattan), *O'Henry's Full House* (1952), in which he played opposite the late Oscar Levant and Fred Allen, and *Hondo* (1953). He had the title role in *Benjy*, which won an Oscar as the Best Documentary Short of 1951. His one big disappointment came when he tested for *Shane* and was promised the part only to learn a few days later that it had been given instead to the late Brandon de Wilde.

The money he was paid in salaries and residuals was invested for him in real estate and stocks.

For a few years, he was a production assistant for the TV series *Route 66*. He spent a year in Mexico and another one touring Europe. For the two years he was married, Lee and his wife lived in northern California.

Although he has no close contacts with the movie industry and says he doesn't miss it, neither does he completely rule out acting again. Aaker shares a Redondo Beach apartment with three dogs and a young woman. He is a carpenter.

He lives with a young woman in Hermosa Beach. Lee earns his living as a carpenter.

In 1945 Paige was under contract to Universal Pictures.

ROBERT PAIGE

The Hollywood leading man and TV host was born on December 21, 1910, in Indianapolis, Indiana, to English parents. He is related to Admiral David Beatty, hero of the World War I Battle of Jutland. His real name is John A. Page.

Using the name Dave Carlyle, Paige first worked in radio on a Long Beach station. A studio scout got him a test at Columbia, where he was put under contract for a year. Later he spent a year at Warner Brothers, two years at Paramount and was with Universal for three years.

DEANNA... in her best TECHNICOLOR triumph!

with the Miracle Melodies of JEROME KERN!

Deanna DURBIN

CAN'T HELP SINGING

in TECHNICOLOR

with ROBERT PAIGE
AKIM TAMIROFF

DAVID BRUCE   LEONID KINSKEY   RAY COLLINS   JUNE VINCENT   ANDREW TOMBES   THOMAS GOMEZ

Paige's debut was in the Marion Davies starrer *Cain and Mabel* (1936). He seldom made an "A" feature. His big chance was supposed to come in *Can't Help Singing* (1944), in which he sang a duet "Californ-i-ay" with Deanna Durbin. At the time, she was one of the most popular stars in pictures. It failed to put him over, though.

Although he was never really bad in movies, neither was he individual enough to register strongly. He admits that he is probably best remembered for the two films he made with Abbott and Costello, *Pardon My Sarong* (1941) and *Abbott and Costello Go to Mars* (1953). He strongly objected to making both at the time.

He was also seen in *The Main Event* (1938), *Golden Gloves* (1940) with Jeanne Cagney (divorced and living in Newport Beach, California), *The Monster and the Girl* (1941) with Philip Terry (living in Los Angeles) and *Her Primitive Man* (1944). His co-star in the latter was Louise Allbritton (married to CBS newsman Charles Collingwood and living in Puerto Vallarta, Mexico). The two were teamed in a series of light comedies.

While on tour to promote *Red Stallion* (1947), he met oil millionaire Glenn McCarthy, who financed *The Green Promise* (1949), which Paige produced. His last acting roles were in *The Marriage-Go-Round* (1960) and *Bye Bye Birdie* (1963).

Fired Wife (1943) was one of a series of comedies Robert made opposite Louise Allbritton. She is now the wife of CBS newsman Charles Collingwood.

In the 1950's, Paige turned to TV as the host of the *Schlitz Playhouse* for two seasons. Then he emceed *Bride and Groom* in 1957. His greatest exposure was co-hosting *The Big Payoff* in 1962 with Bess Myerson. From 1966 to 1970, he was the newscaster over Channel 7 in Los Angeles.

Bob is now a Deputy Supervisor of the County of Los Angeles. (Henry Koster)

In 1960 he divorced his wife of twenty years and two years later married Joanne Ludden, the model on *The Big Payoff.* They live in Beverly Hills with their daughter Colleen.

Robert is now a deputy to Baxter Ward, Los Angeles County's most independent and controversial supervisor. One of the few people he sees from his movie-making days is Andy Devine , an old and close friend.

He has total recall of his career and loves telling stories. One of his favorites is a detailed account of the affair he had with a young singing star. Says Paige, "She was publicized all over the world as being lady-like and very pure. If the public only knew!"

HIGHLIGHTS

1910   Born on December 21 in Indianapolis, Indiana.

1936   Made his movie debut in *Cain and Mabel.*

1944   Played opposite Deanna Durbin.

1950-60   Was host and emcee on various network TV shows.

1963   Made *Bye Bye Birdie,* his last film.

1966-70   Reported news over Channel 7 in Los Angeles.

1970   Became Deputy to Los Angeles County Supervisor.

Anne signed a contract beginning at $75.00 a week with Universal Pictures in June of 1939.

ANNE GWYNNE

The movie actress and popular pin-up girl of World War II was born Marguerite Gwynne Trice in Waco, Texas, on December 10, 1918.

The summer before she was to enter her sophomore year at Stephens College, Anne accompanied her father to a convention in Los Angeles. He was with Catalina Swimwear, and she got a job modeling bathing suits. This led to a part in a little theatre production. Soon she was making the rounds of studios and agents' offices.

The July, 1944 issue of *Photoplay* magazine had Anne in a tie-in advertisement for one of her pictures.

Lewis Stone, who played Mickey Rooney's father in the *Andy Hardy* series, was one of the guests at Anne's wedding to an attorney in 1945. Her bridesmaid was Evelyn Ankers, who is still a close friend.

One day she had appointments at Universal in the morning and at Warner Brothers after lunch. Anne never made it to her second date. After a 30-minute interview, she was signed to a contract which began at $75.00 a week in June of 1939.

Even though she didn't have a single line in a short she made with Edgar Bergen[2] and Charlie McCarthy, fans noticed her and wrote in asking who she was. Anne's appeal was very visual.

Her relatively low salary, combined with her willingness to pose for endless hours of cheesecake photography, made her a favorite in the front office. Her reward, however, was to be overworked in one "B" picture after another:

Unexpected Father (1939) with Baby Sandy,[5] *Mob Town* (1941) with Dick Foran (living in Van Nuys, California), *The Glass Alibi* (1942), *Frontier Badmen* (1943), *Murder in the Blue Room* (1944) and *Dick Tracy Meets Gruesome* (1947). In one year alone, she had the lead in 13 features.

She was also in two Deanna Durbin movies, *Spring Parade* (1940) and *Nice Girl* (1941), and was a bridesmaid at the star's wedding.

It was Anne's ability to emit blood-curdling screams that has kept her a familiar face to movie fans over the years. She was seen and heard shrieking her lungs out in horror pictures that are still popular: *Black Friday* (1940), *The Black Cat* (1941) with the late Claire Dodd, *The Strange Case of Doctor Rx* (1942), *The House of Frankenstein* (1944), *Weird Woman* (1944) and *The Ghost Goes Wild* (1947). Two of her other films that remain favorites on TV are *Flash Gordon Conquers the Universe* (1940) and *Ride 'Em Cowboy* (1942) with Abbott[2] and Costello.

When Anne married a theatrical lawyer-producer in 1945, Evelyn Ankers was her maid of honor. The two still correspond. Another close friend from the old days, whom she still sees, is Lois Collier (married to a Beverly Hills attorney). Her daughter, Gwynne Gilford and her husband, Robert Pine, both act on TV. Anne is a grandmother by her son.

Widowed since 1965, Anne lives alone in the San Fernando Valley. To keep herself occupied, she does secretarial work for a metaphysician.

She would very much like to act again, but a bit part in *Adam at 6 AM* (1970) has been her only role in a long time. She speaks wistfully of her career: "I wish I had been more insistent on better pictures. Maria Montez complained about absolutely everything and told me not to be so cooperative. They made her a star, and I'm sure her demands had a lot to do with it. It was a busy, happy time in my life, and I have no regrets, but I must admit that every now and then I wonder what might have happened if I'd kept that appointment at Warners."

Today Anne Gwynne is the secretary to a metaphysician in the San Fernando Valley. (Michael Knowles)

In 1935 Paramount Pictures chose these six young ladies as their "Most Likely to Succeed." Clockwise from bottom left are: Katherine De Mille, the late Ann Sheridan, Gail Patrick,[5] Wendy Barrie, the late Gertrude Michael and Grace Bradley (the widow of Bill "Hopalong Cassidy" Boyd lives in Palm Desert).

Paramount dubbed these five young hopefuls "The Golden Circle". From left to right are: the late Susan Hayward, the late Joseph Allen, Ellen Drew (retired, married and living in Palm Desert), Robert Preston and the late Betty Grable.

Before coming to Paramount Betty Grable had been dropped by both Samuel Goldwyn (who changed her name to Frances Dean) and RKO. Shortly after this photo was taken in 1939 Paramount, too, let her go. But by 1943 she had become Twentieth-Century Fox's biggest star and was named by LIFE magazine that year's Number One Box-Office Attraction. She died on July 2, 1973.

By the mid-'30s, Katherine had left 20th Century-Fox studios and joined Paramount Pictures, where her husband, Anthony Quinn, was under contract and her father, Cecil B. De Mille, had his own unit.

KATHERINE DE MILLE

The screen beauty of the 1930's was born Katherine Lester on June 29, 1911, in Vancouver, B.C. After her Canadian father was killed during the Battle of Verdun, her mother, who was Swiss-German, brought her to Los Angeles. By 1920, Katherine's mother had died of tuberculosis and she was placed in an orphanage.

She was adopted by Cecil B. De Mille and his wife, who was a director of the orphan asylum. It was, however, her friends, the late Mischa Auer[1] and Frank Tuttle, who encouraged her to act. Her adoptive father never even suggested a movie career to her. She began as an extra and worked her way into bit parts. An early one was in De Mille's production of *Madame Satan* (1930) with Kay Johnson (divorced and living in Waterford, Connecticut).

When director George Cukor suggested she get some stage experience, she went to the Berkshire Playhouse. Katherine did so well she was offered the title role in the London production of *The Trial of Mary Dugan*. Instead, she chose to sign a contract with the Fox studios. Three years later she moved to Paramount, her father's home lot.

Before Katherine made up her mind to act in movies she worked as an assistant to her father, producer-director Cecil B. DeMille, on his early talkie *The Squawman* (1931).

Katherine claims that her father took special pains to keep his hands off her career and that he was very hard on her when they worked together. A contemporary who was on the set of *The Crusades* (1935) remembers their relationship quite differently. According to him, De Mille spent more time seeing that his daughter was well photographed than he did directing the picture's star, Loretta Young.

Her other credits include: *Belle of the Nineties* (1934), *Call of the Wild* (1935), *Ramona* (1936), *Blockade* (1938) and *Aloma of the South Seas* (1941).

The first turning point in her adult life came on March 16, 1941. She had been married to Anthony Quinn for four years when their three-year-old son, Christopher, wandered off his grandparents' estate and onto a neighboring property, which was rented by W. C. Fields. The boy fell into a lily pond and drowned. The comedian, who had a well-publicized reputation for disliking children, was very disturbed by the tragedy and moved away almost immediately.

One of the few pictures she made after her son's death was *Unconquered* (1947), which her father directed.

The second jolt came in 1964, when she and Quinn were divorced. The actor had fathered two children by an Italian actress who later became his wife.

Although Katherine lives in Pacific Palisades, she sees virtually no one from the movie colony. "I always was a spectator of the Hollywood scene," she said recently. "I found it very unreal on the surface and I sensed a nightmare beneath."

She is the mother of a son and three daughters. Most of her time is spent either teaching Bible classes at a Presbyterian church or doing social work in ghetto areas. "I like to be involved with people in need," says Katherine.

Her son by Anthony Quinn was seven months old when this photo was taken. On March 16, 1941, the boy, who was then four years old, fell into W. C. Fields' lily pond and drowned.

Ms. De Mille never remarried after her divorce from Anthony Quinn. She devotes most of her time to teaching Bible classes and doing social work in ghetto areas.

MILESTONES

1911 Born on June 29 in Vancouver, B.C., Canada

1920 Adopted by Cecil B. De Mille

1930 Began doing bit parts in movies

1937 Married Anthony Quinn

1941 Son drowned in W. C. Fields' lily pond

1964 Divorced from Quinn

"YOUNG WIDDER BROWN"

"The story of the age-old conflict between a mother's duty and a woman's heart" began over the Mutual Broadcasting Company in 1937. Its original title was *Young Widder Jones*, which was changed shortly after its debut because of a conflict with a product's name. During the first thirty-nine weeks the *"Widder's"* major problem was a debt of $24.00 incurred in opening her bake shop. The theme song in those days was *"In the Gloaming."*

In 1940, the cast of *Young Widder Brown* was: (seated, left to right) "Marjorie Williams" Toni Gilman, "Mark Brown" Tommy Donnelly, "Young Widder Brown" Florance Freeman, "Jane Brown" Marilyn Erskine, "Maria Hawkins" Agnes Young. (standing left to right): Announcer George Ansbro, "Victoria Loring" Rita Royce, "Dr. Anthony Loring," Ned Wever and the director, Martha Atwell. (NBC photo)

On September 26, 1938, the fifteen-minute, five-times-a-week program moved to the NBC Red Network. There *Ellen Brown* ran a tea shop in *Simpsonville*.

As her popularity grew, so did her troubles. But not her two children, who always seemed to remain the same age. When Florence Freeman, who originated the title role, posed for publicity photos, the show's producers, Frank and Anne Hummert, hired models as her children. The actors playing the parts on the air were considered "too old-looking" for the image the sponsors wanted for the *Brown* family. On the air, her boy *Mark* was played by Tommy Donnelly. His sister *Janey* was Marilyn Erskine.

The title role was originated by Florence Freeman, who played it until 1953. (NBC photo)

Early in the story, Ellen's complicated love life took a turn that was not planned. The late Bud Collyer played the character of a young doctor who became engaged to the widowed *Mrs. Brown*. During their courtship it was learned that he was already married but that his wife was insane. The writers made the mistake of having his wife come home for a visit. When the Hummerts learned that she had been in her estranged husband's home overnight, Ellen's fiance was immediately written out of the script forever.

Her next beau was *Dr. Anthony Loring*, who was always played by Ned Wever. He was to her what *Gil Whitney* was to radio's *Helen Trent*. For all the heartbreaks, mishaps and misunderstandings, listeners knew that he was the man for Ellen. On the final broadcast, June 29, 1956, they were being married as the theme *Wonderful One* was heard for the last time.

The show's main writer Elizabeth Todd is dead as is its director, Martha Atwell. George Ansbro, the announcer for almost all of its years on the air, lives in Montclair, New Jersey. Ned Wever, who still acts occasionally, is a realtor in Laguna Hills, California. He had also been heard for many years on radio as *Dick Tracy* and *Bulldog Drummond*.

Florence Freeman left the series after the Thanksgiving Day broadcast of 1953 and was replaced by Wendy Drew. Along with being *Ellen Brown*, she played the title role of *Wendy Warren and the News* for the full twelve years it was on the air. At the time her departure was said to be "by mutual consent." Twenty years later, however, Ms. Freeman revealed that the producers told her that she had lost "that young feeling." The actress who played the part for over sixteen years recently described it as "corny" and said that the program had "a basically false premise." In a recent interview, she was especially piqued at her lack of billing all those years: "The only time they ever mentioned my name on the air was when I was sick. Then they thanked whatever actress had taken over for me."

Florence Freeman is married to a rabbi and now lives in Jersey City, New Jersey. (Kendra Erwin-Kerr)

Ned Wever, who played "Dr. Anthony Loring" for 17 years, lives in Laguna Hills, California. (Bob Lopez)

Frank's specialty was always his high-pitched, delirious laughter. In 1937, when this photo was taken, he had been under contract to Warner Brothers for seven years.

FRANK McHUGH

The character actor of stage and movies was born on May 23, 1899, in Homestead, Pennsylvania. He made his debut in a play with his parents in 1909. Frank received invaluable training during the years he spent in stock companies, a minstrel show and road tours. He was first seen on Broadway in *The Fall Guy* (1925). Then he was with Jimmy Gleason in the London company of *Is Zat So?* (1926). His appearance with the late Miriam Hopkins in *Excess Baggage* (1927) gave his career a big boost. Flo Ziegfeld had him in *Show Girl* (1929).

In 1930, Frank signed a contract with Warner Brothers, where he stayed for ten years. His wise-cracking fit perfectly into their big-city, fast-talking pictures of the period. He played in as many as thirteen features in one year. A few of his better ones were: *Little Caesar* (1930), *The Front Page* (1931), *One Way Passage* (1932), *A Midsummer Night's Dream* (1935), *Three Men on a Horse* (1936), *Boy Meets Girl* (1938), *Dodge City* (1939) and *Manpower* (1941).

The parts he played most often were as a priest, the second to a prize fighter and the smart-aleck reporter. McHugh the actor was famous for his delirious laughter and for appearing inebriated. McHugh the man has an excellent sense of humor but hasn't had a drink since 1937.

He freelanced right up until his last picture, *Easy Come, Easy Go* (1967), with the late Allen Jenkins.[4] Some that came before were: *Going My Way* (1944), *State Fair* (1945), *The Mighty Joe Young* (1949), *A Lion is in the Streets*

Another Warner Brothers contract player, Loretta Young, gives Frank the word in this 1931 publicity still.

(1953), *There's No Business Like Show Business* (1954), *The Last Hurrah* (1958) and *A Tiger Walks* (1963).

During the 1950's he did a lot of television drama. In 1964 he had a running part on Bing Crosby's short-lived TV series.

In 1962 Frank replaced the late David Burns in *A Funny Thing Happened on My Way to the Forum* on Broadway.

Joan Blondell and Frank got star billing in *Three Men on a Horse* (1936).

He was supposed to play Ruby Keeler's husband in the 1971 production of *No, No Nanette* but was fired before the hit show made its Broadway bow. McHugh had taken over for the ailing Hiram Sherman at the last minute. He had very little rehearsal but consented to go on during the out-of-town tryouts anyway. When producer Cyma Rubin replaced him in spite of his run-of-the-play contract, he took the matter to Actors Equity. The musical's stars, Ruby

Keeler and Patsy Kelly, old pals of his since the 1920's, testified in his behalf. Frank won a sizeable settlement.

Since 1950, Frank and his wife of over forty years have lived in Cos Cob, Connecticut. Their twenty-year-old son was killed in an auto crash in 1955. They have another boy and a girl. McHugh spends much of his time gardening and reading law. He is still close to his friend of almost fifty years, Jimmy Cagney.[4] Asked recently if he was retired, Frank replied, "No, I'm just out of work."

Frank and his wife of over forty years live in Cos Cob, Connecticut. He is still close to his long-time friend, Jimmy Cagney. (Jon Virzi)

MILESTONES

1898   Born on May 23rd in Homestead, Pennsylvania

1909   Debuted on stage with parents

1925   Made Broadway debut in *The Fall Guy*

1929   Appeared in Ziegfeld's *Show Girl*

1930   Began a ten-year stay at Warner Brothers

1955   Son was killed in an auto crash

1967   Made last movie, *Easy Come, Easy Go*

1971   Fired from *No, No Nanette*

WENDY BARRIE

The British movie actress and television personality was born Marguerite Wendy Jenkin in Hong Kong on April 18, 1912. Her father was one of the original team of barristers who represented the famed murderer Crippen. Her Irish mother took the name "Wendy" from her favorite story, *Peter Pan*.* Ms. Barrie was educated at schools in England and Switzerland.

Wendy began acting as a lark, but by the time her first London play, *Wonderbar*, had closed, she had decided on a theatrical career.

* Her last name came from its author, Sir James Barrie.

Wendy came to the U.S. in 1934. She always felt she "had flopped in Hollywood."

Spencer Tracy and Wendy were in *It's A Small World* (1935).

Playing Jane Seymour in the highly successful picture *The Private Life of Henry VIII* (1933) made her a name overnight. She might have stayed in England had it not been for a romance with the five-and-ten-cent-store heir Woolworth Donohue. Her fiancé brought her to his mother for her blessing. When Mrs. Donohue disapproved of the match, Wendy consoled herself by coming to Hollywood. The year was 1934.

In later years, Ms. Barrie refused to discuss her American films. Her feeling that she "had flopped in Hollywood" is not wholly true. She is fondly remembered by many for her role of the spoiled, rich girl in *Dead End* (1937). *The Hound of the Baskervilles* (1939), however, is her only other Hollywood movie of any consequence.

In 1936 she made *Speed* with Jimmy Stewart.

Her first picture in this country was *It's a Small World* (1935) with Spencer Tracy. Some of the others were *A Feather in Her Hat* (1935) with Louis Hayward,[5] *Breezing Home* (1937) with William Gargan[5] and *Men Against the Sky* (1940). She was the female lure in three of the filmed adventures of "The Saint" and two of "The Falcon" features, including the first, *The Gay Falcon* (1941). The late George Sanders played the title roles in all five. Her last for a long time were in 1943: *Forever and a Day* and *Submarine Alert* with Richard Arlen (living in the San Fernando Valley).

In May of 1948, Wendy was married to an industrialist and virtually retired when she guested on a TV show. From that appearance, she was hired to host a kiddie series called *Okey Dokey Ranch*. The expression "Be a good bunny," which she began using on that program, became her signature for the remainder of her career.

Wendy played Jane Seymour, the third wife of Charles Laughton, in the movie classic *The Private Life of Henry VIII* (1933).

In 1954, she got a divorce and made a brief return to movie acting when she appeared as herself in *It Should Happen to You*. By then, she was well established as a talk-show host both on radio and television. She was associated for a while in the 1950's with Revlon, but she left after a disagreement with its late founder, Charles Revson.

Wendy became ill in 1970. At the time, she was hosting her own syndicated interview program that she recorded at New York's Hotel Biltmore. It was carried by over three hundred radio stations. Since then, she has been living in a nursing home in Manhattan. Ms. Barrie has no known relatives.

Wendy made two "Falcon" features with George Sanders. He committed suicide on April 25, 1972.

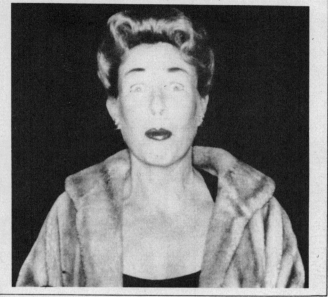

Wendy clowning for the camera. This photo was taken shortly before she became ill. (Jon Virzi)

MILESTONES

1912 Born on April 18 in Hong Kong

1933 Played Jane Seymour in the hit movie *The Private Life of Henry VIII.*

1934 Came to the U.S. to marry five and ten cent store heir. Went instead to Hollywood.

1945 Married an industrialist and retired

1948 Made a comeback as TV host

1970 Left the air because of illness

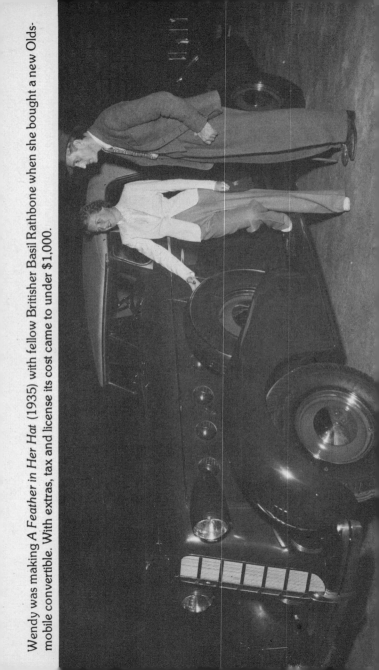

Wendy was making *A Feather in Her Hat* (1935) with fellow Britisher Basil Rathbone when she bought a new Oldsmobile convertible. With extras, tax and license its cost came to under $1,000.

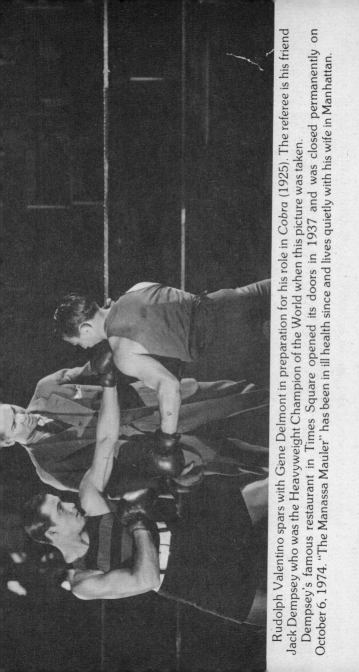

Rudolph Valentino spars with Gene Delmont in preparation for his role in *Cobra* (1925). The referee is his friend Jack Dempsey who was the Heavyweight Champion of the World when this picture was taken. Dempsey's famous restaurant in Times Square opened its doors in 1937 and was closed permanently on October 6, 1974. "The Manassa Mauler" has been in ill health since and lives quietly with his wife in Manhattan.

DICK FORAN

Warner Brothers billed Foran in his Westerns as "The Singing Cowboy." In one he introduced the song, *I'll Remember April.*

The Western star and leading man of movies was born John Nicholas Foran in Flemington, New Jersey, on June 18, 1910. His father, who was a state senator, sent him to Mercersburg Academy and then to Princeton. Dick was an all-around athlete at both.

After graduation, he went to work as an investigator for the Pennsylvania Railroad. One of his assignments brought him in contact with Lew Brown of the producing and songwriting team of DeSylva, Brown and Henderson. They persuaded him to take a screen test.

Fox Studios signed him, and he made *Stand Up and Cheer* (1934) and a few others. The next year he moved over to Warner Brothers for a long stay.

His new studio used him mostly as the lead in programmers and as a supporting player in "A" features. Midway in his career, Warner publicists began referring to him as Richard Foran in a vain attempt to strengthen his image.

Dick's features were perfect for the Irish policeman he played in *Easy Come, Easy Go* (1947).

The only time Foran really came off well was in Westerns. George N. Fenin and William K. Everson, in their book *The Western,* described him as "not only vastly superior to Autry as a singer, but he was a much better actor at dramatics and action as well, and his Westerns had exceptionally high production values." Billed as "The Singing Cowboy," Dick sang "My Little Buckaroo," a hit of the time, in *Cherokee Strip* (1937). In *Ride 'Em Cowboy* (1942), he introduced "I'll Remember April," which is now regarded as a standard.

Some of his other appearances were in *The Petrified Forest* (1936), *Guns of the Pecos* (1937) with the late Anne Nagel, *Boy Meets Girl* (1938), *My Little Chickadee* (1940), *Guest Wife* (1945), *Fort Apache* (1948), *Treasure of Ruby Hill* (1955), *Studs Lonigan* (1960) and *Brighty of the Grand Canyon* (1968). He also starred in two serials and was seen on Broadway in the revival of *A Connecticut Yankee in King Arthur's Court* in 1943.

Foran's first two marriages were to actresses and were unsuccessful. During his second divorce, newspapers carried accounts of his wife's testimony, in which she accused him of attempting to poison her. His third wife was described at the time of their marriage as "a socialite."

Dick raises Weimaraners at his home in Van Nuys. His wife is studying for her doctorate. Their son, Tommy, who is eight years old, has appeared on a TV commercial. Foran has been inactive as an actor since his successful bout with skin cancer several years ago, but he is working on a book of his experiences in Hollywood, tentatively called *A Rock is a Rock, a Tree is a Tree.*

Dick played the husband of Gale Page in Warner's *Four Daughters* series. Gale lives in Los Angeles, where this was taken recently. (Jon Virzi)

He lives now in Van Nuys with his wife and their young son. (Jon Virzi)

This photo was taken at the Warner Brothers studio commissary in 1938. (Far side of table, from left to right): Screenwriter Julius Epstein, Gale Page, Dick Foran, director Michael Curtiz, cameraman Ernie Haller and Lola Lane. (Near side of table): Director Irving Rapper, the late Rosemary Lane, George Brent‡ and Priscilla Lane.

The personalities photographed on the Paramount lot in 1933 are (from left to right): Kathleen "The Panther Woman" Burke, director Norman Z. McLeod, Stuart Erwin, Allison Skipworth, Jack Oakie, Brian Aherne, Wynne Gibson, director Wesley Ruggles, Richard Arlen, Carole Lombard, Adrienne Ames, Fredric March, Charles Starrett,[5] Charles Ruggles, Randolph Scott and Nancy Carroll.

WYNNE GIBSON

Wynne's part in *If I Had a Million*, in which she played a street prostitute, was censored from showings in most states when it was originally released in 1932.

The star of early talkies was born in New York City on July 3. Although she had no training or experience in acting, she was determined to go into the theatre. When her family tried to dissuade her, Wynne ran away from home.

She was only 15 years old when she landed a

part in *Tangerine* (1922). The stars of the play were Jimmy Gleason and Jeanette MacDonald. After some coaching by Lew Fields of the famed comedy team of Weber and Fields, Wynne toured the vaudeville houses. Her partners in that act were Billie Vernon, the wife of Jimmy Cagney,[1] and Ray Raymond.[*] Then she was on Broadway with Jack Whiting in *When You Smile* (1925).

Her portrayal of a drunk in the 1928 production of *Jarnegan* convinced an agent that she was right for pictures. Wynne was getting a divorce at the time and welcomed the chance to make some money and to try her luck in Hollywood.

After signing an MGM contract, she made one programmer and was then cast in an "A" picture. When word reached her that the picture's star did not want her in it, Wynne asked for her release. "Louis B. Mayer told me I was crazy," she said recently. "Of course, he was absolutely right. I have always been my own worst enemy."

---

[*]Raymond, a musical comedy star, was killed by actor Paul Kelly in a fight over the effections of Raymond's wife, Dorothy MacKaye. Kelly served two years in prison after he was convicted of manslaughter in a highly publicized trial in 1927. He and Ms. MacKaye had been married for nine years when she was killed in a car crash in 1940 on the anniversary of the crime. Kelly died in November of 1956.

Her appearance in the title role of *Molly Mag-dalene* in a Los Angeles theatre got her a contract with Paramount. Wynne was cast opposite Gary Cooper, William Powell and John Gilbert; she stole the notices from Clara Bow in *Kick-In* (1931) and was with Mae West in her film debut, *Night After Night* (1932). Yet she is probably best known among film buffs for the episodic *If I Had a Million*. Her sequence, in which she played a street prositute who inherits a fortune, was censored from most showings in the United States when it was released in 1932. Although it invariably gets a big hand when screened at revivals, Wynne's deliciously risque performance is still being edited from the prints shown by some TV stations.

Beverly Roberts and Wynne have been good friends since they met while making *Flirting with Fate* in 1938. The picture's star was the late Joe E. Brown.

Today Ms. Roberts heads Theatre Authority in New York City. (Jon Virzi)

When she went with RKO, it was with the hope that she would be cast in something other than the part of a "tough blonde dame." Wynne feels she was "sold down the river" professionally. The studio loaned her out to other lots without any discrimination as to the parts she would be playing.

Her career still might have been saved if Stephen Roberts had lived. The director had promised to star her in *Valiant is the Word for Carrie*. After his death, the part went to Gladys George, who made a great success with it.

Ms. Gibson made a couple of pictures in England and then returned for *Come Closer, Folks* (1936) with Marian Marsh (married to the millionaire aviation pioneer Clifford Henderson. They live in Palm Springs). Until she quit movies in the mid-forties, Wynne worked in such low-budget features as *Trapped by G-Men* (1937), *Street of Missing Women* (1940) and *The Falcon Strikes Back* (1943).

In 1945, Ms. Gibson moved to New York City and formed a partnership with Beverly Roberts to produce a play. Nothing ever came of it, but they have been close friends ever since. The two had met while making *Flirting with Fate* (1938), a Joe E. Brown movie. Ms. Roberts heads Theatre Authority in New York. They share a large house on Long Island. Wynne still keeps in touch with her old friend, Mae Clarke.[4]

During the out-of-town tryouts of *Annie Get Your Gun* (1946), Wynne found that her role got smaller each week at the insistence of the musical's star. On opening night in Boston, she gave her notice to Richard Rodgers, who commented, "I can hardly blame you."

Since then she has appeared in running parts on radio and TV in such soap operas as *When a Girl Marries*, *Valiant Lady* and *Love of Life*.

Although she is no longer represented by an agent, she candidly admits that she has no desire to retire: "I'm old enough and free enough to do the kinds of things Marie Dressler played in. I'd just love to work again."

MILESTONES

1922 Runs away from home at age 15 and lands a part in a Broadway play

1928 Signs an MGM contract

1929 Quits Metro, joins Paramount

1932 Plays street prostitute in *If I Had a Million*

1934 Moves to RKO, where she is "sold down the river"

1946 Leaves cast of *Annie Get Your Gun* before it opens on Broadway

Wynne would like to play the kind of parts Marie Dressler specialized in. (Gawain Bierne-Keyt)

TEDDY NADLER

The contestant who became the biggest money winner of all—$264,000—during the TV quiz show mania of the 1950's was born in St. Louis on December 15, 1909. His father, who was a shoemaker, was out of work most of the time, and his mother was an invalid. Teddy and his five brothers and sisters spent much of their childhoods in the Jewish Shelter Home.

Emcee Ralph Storey with Teddy in August of 1958. After this photo was taken he won another $12,000 for a grand total of $264,000. (U.P.I.)

Nadler escaped the harsh realities of the orphanage by reading everything he could get his hands on. Although he did not go to school beyond the eighth grade, he continued memorizing books until he was 22 years old. At that age, he stopped reading entirely.

His phenomenal memory, which permits him to name 3,000 generals, 2,000 assassinations, 10,000 battles and 2,000 kings as well as every island on earth, was of little help to him before and after his appearances on *The $64,000 Question* and *The $64,000 Challenge.* During the many years he spent as a civilian clerk at an Army Depot, he was unable to get a promotion. His bosses and co-workers took little notice of his command of facts since his English is poor and his pronunciation often garbled.

After his first appearance on network television in July of 1956, he became a national hero. Millions sat before their TV sets spellbound as the little man astonished and, at times, angered the world experts he was pitted against. He seemed to know the Civil War as well as he knew great and obscure composers. Not only did he remember all of the kings of France, but he also could recite them backwards, including their births, deaths and the years of their reigns. The press dubbed him "Mr. Know It All." Teachers and parents held him up to children as an example of the rewards of study.

Taxes took $160,000 of his winnings. He now lives in a small, uncarpeted apartment. His three sons have left home, and Teddy lives with his wife who, he says, "knows nothing about anything." He summed up his marriage recently by saying, "We have absolutely nothing in common." He admits that most people prefer his wife, however, to him. "I can understand why," says Nadler. "Who wants to hear me rattle off the births and deaths of ancient kings? And that's all I can do. That and worry, which is how I spend my time." He says he worries mainly about money. Although neither he nor his wife bought any luxuries or traveled with their windfall, Nadler maintains that most of his winnings are gone. He has tried repeatedly to get a job, but he says no one will hire him. In 1960, he applied to become a census taker but flunked the test.

Nadler has not worked a day since he won his money. He lives in a modest apartment in Olivette, Missouri. (Shifra Haran)

Although he refers to himself as "the greatest" and "the eighth wonder of the world," he speaks of his total recall as if it were a terrible burden. Baseball, one of his fields of *expertise*, is a sport that does not even interest him. It angers him that he retains thousands of scores and batting averages. "Maybe I could sleep at night if I didn't have all this stuff running through my mind," he says. "Maybe I wouldn't have this ulcer."

"The Human Computer" has very little ability at mathematics and says his philosophy of life is "getting through the day." The memory that allows him to quote entire Shakespearean plays does not retain dates and facts about his own family. He admits that he often looks everywhere for his car keys, only to find that they were in his hand all along. Said an interviewer who spent several hours with him: "Nadler knows almost everything and understands almost nothing."

JUNIOR COGHLAN

The child star of silents and early talkies was born in New Haven, Connecticut, on March 15, 1916.

When the Coghlans moved to Hollywood, their only child was three years old. His parents were both working as extras in films when someone suggested that they try to get Junior into pictures. At the time, he had his hair cut in bangs, a fashion of the day popularized by Jackie Coogan.

Junior's first film role was a part in the Clara Kimball Young starrer *To Please One Woman* (1921). He then appeared in a few *Our Gang* comedies.

Bessie Love with Junior in a scene from *Rubber Tires* (1927). Ms. Love lives in London, where she is still active in films and on stage.

Coghlan played "Billy Batson," the boy who was transformed into "Captain Marvel" by the word "Shazam." Tom Tyler, who played "Captain Marvel" in the 1941 serial, died on May 1, 1954.

Director Marshall Neilan brought him to the attention of Cecil B. DeMille, who was looking for a boy to play an important role in *The Road to Yesterday* (1925). Neilan used him in *Sky Rocket* (1926) and *Mike* (1926). Both men were impressed with how easily Coghlan took direction. He became the only child DeMille ever had under contract.

Because his voice was somewhat high, it seemed, for a while, that he would not be suitable for talkies. Then he was cast in *Penrod and Sam* (1931), which did very well at the box office. He played "Sam" to Leon Janney's "Penrod." After that picture, he found plenty of work.

Junior's sound credits include *River's End* (1931) with Evalyn Knapp (widowed and living in West Hollywood), *Union Depot* (1932), *Hell's House* (1932), one of Bette Davis' earliest pictures, *Make Way for a Lady* (1936) with Anne Shirley[5] and *The Last of the Mohicans,* a 1932 serial.

As he came out of his teens, his billing changed to Frank Coghlan, Jr., but it didn't help him much with parts. He was Mickey Rooney's pal, "Red," in a couple of "Andy Hardy" features and played a soda jerk in *Meet Dr. Christian* (1939). Only three years before, he had been co-starred with Dickie Moore (who now heads up his own public-relations firm in New York City) in *Little Red Schoolhouse* (1936). When he joined the Navy in 1941 Coghlan didn't leave much of a career.

Coghlan did not return to civilian life for twenty-three years. He was in Hollywood, however, for the last five years of his tour of duty, acting as liaison officer between the film studios and the Navy.

Although he has done commercials occasionally and small parts in movies, Frank has been steadily employed as the public-relations director for the Los Angeles City Zoo for several years.

All five of his children have worked on TV or in movies. After his first wife died a few years ago, he married a widow who also has five children. They live in Sepulveda, California.

Anita Louise was the girl Junior won in *Square Shoulders*. She died on April 25, 1970.

Frank is well aware that he is best known for his role of "Billy Batson," the boy who could change into "Captain Marvel" by saying "Shazam." He and Billy Benedict, another cast member of the 1941 serial, *The Adventures of Captain Marvel*, appear now and then at film-buff conventions around the country.

Coghlan recently told an interviewer about his father's heavy drinking and gambling. "He was embarrassed that I made so much money," explained Frank. "It was my money that put him through school to become a chiropractor. I was glad I could do it. But he kept right on until we lost the apartment house we were buying. By the time I was twenty-one I was not only broke but deeply in debt because of my dad. My compensation was having the world's greatest mother."

Because he went to public schools most of the time, he did not find the transition to life in the service as difficult as did some child stars.

He says he liked everyone he ever worked with and was never terribly disappointed when he lost out on a movie role. "It was always a job to me," said the soft-spoken Coghlan. "A good job, but a job."

deLacy is an advertising executive in Los Angeles. (Joel Preisler)

He still sees some of the child actors with whom he worked, such as Philippe deLacy (an advertising executive in Los Angeles) and Gene Reynolds (a successful Hollywood producer). He is still close to Jackie Cooper, his co-star in the 1939 serial *Scouts to the Rescue*, and Mary Ann Jackson (a divorcee working in a children's shop in Los Angeles) of *Our Gang*.

One of his prized possessions is a baseball signed to him by Lou Gehrig and Babe Ruth, whom he met during the filming of *Slide, Kelly, Slide* (1927). One of the social highlights of his Hollywood days was his date with Bonita Granville. It was the first time her mother let a boy take her out.

When Frank joined the Navy, he had not seen the "Captain Marvel" serial he had just completed. When it played in then segregated Pensacola, Florida, while he was stationed there, it was in an all-black theatre. At first, he was refused admittance. Finally, the white manager permitted him to enter after he agreed to watch the film from the very last row.

Frank is in charge of public relations for the Los Angeles Zoo. He and his first wife had five children. After her death he married a widow with five children.

MILESTONES

1916 Born on March 15, in New Haven, Connecticut

1921 Debuts in a Clara Kimball Young feature film

1925 Becomes the only child ever to be under contract to Cecil B. DeMille

1931 Makes successful transition to talkies in *Penrod and Sam*

1941 Begins a 23-year hitch in the Navy

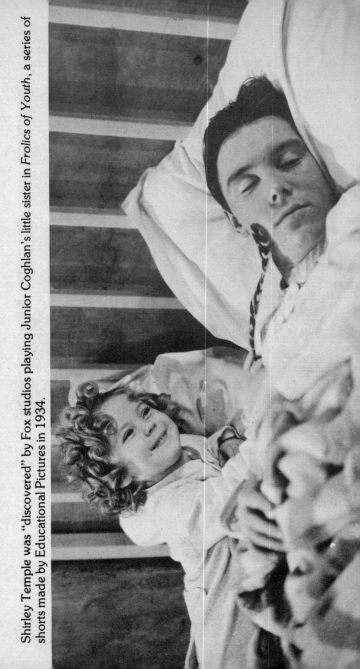

Shirley Temple was "discovered" by Fox studios playing Junior Coghlan's little sister in *Frolics of Youth*, a series of shorts made by Educational Pictures in 1934.

EXTRA

COMPLETE RACING

NIGHT Pictorial

Los Angeles Times

EQUAL RIGHTS

LIBERTY UNDER THE LAW

TRUE INDUSTRIAL FREEDOM

VOL. LVIII   Three Parts—40 Pages   ***   FRIDAY MORNING, JUNE 2, 1939.   Page A

DAILY, FIVE CENTS

LOU NOVA STOPS BAER

Submarine on Bottom Off Britain

Lou Nova and Max Baer as They Weighed in for Their Fight

Max Finished in Eleventh

LOU NOVA

In 1935 Lou Nova was the U.S. and World Amateur Heavyweight Boxing Champion.

The one-time prime contender for the Heavyweight Boxing Crown was born in Los Angeles on March 16, 1915. Both his father and paternal grandfather were classical musicians. Lou was an only child.

In high school and at the University of California at Davis, Nova had outstanding records in track, football and baseball. By the time he was twenty, he had taken every major amateur boxing title in the world. He capped his non-professional career in 1935 when he won the International Amateur Heavyweight title in Paris.

After turning professional in 1936, he won twenty straight bouts before "Slapsie" Maxie Rosenbloom[4] stopped him on June 3, 1938. He then took the next four challengers by knockouts. After that, he faced British Champion Tommy Farr (now an executive with a paint company in Sussex, England). He gave the Welshman such a beating that many felt the bout should have been stopped before it went the full fifteen rounds.

On June 1, 1939, Lou entered the ring as an underdog against Max Baer. He came out the victor by an eleventh-round KO. Three-and-a-half months later, it took Tony Galento[5] fourteen rounds to knock out Nova. Lou refused to congratulate "Two-Ton" Tony after the fight. To this day, he refuses to shake Galento's hand. He referred to him recently as "the dirtiest fighter I've ever come across."

On their rematch on April 4, 1941, Nova again knocked out Baer. This time it took him only eight rounds. Baer's defeat was so decisive that the former champion retired from the ring.

After clobbering Baer twice, Lou became the number one challenger for the World Heavyweight Crown which was then held by

Joe Louis. Sports pages referred to the handsome pugilist as "the great white hope" as the boxing world readied for the title fight. The New York *Journal American's* headline of September 29, 1941, read: "Louis 13-5 over Nova." Still the Brown Bomber was well aware of the beatings Lou had given Farr and Baer. Louis had beaten Farr in 1937, but it had taken him a full fifteen rounds to do it. Nova tells of their night together this way:

Lou in a gag photo to publicize his bout with Tony Galento in 1939. After the fight, which "Two-Ton" Tony won by a knockout, Nova refused to congratulate him. To this day he still will not shake the hand of Galento, whom he refers to as "the dirtiest fighter I've ever come across." (U.P.I.)

"Joe Louis was promoter Lou Jacobs' boy. Jacobs ran Madison Square Garden with an iron hand. That's where we fought. And in the ring with us, we had Arthur Donovan, known as 'the house referee.' Don't get me wrong. Joe Louis was the *best* ever, but I was fighting more than the World's Champ that night."

The fight was stopped with seconds to go and with Nova on the canvas in the sixth round. At that point, Nova says that he was fully conscious and maintains that he was ahead on points on most score cards. He collected a purse of $225,000, his largest ever. America's entry into World War II ruled out the possibility of a rematch.

The following May 25, Lee Savold KO'd

Lou in the eighth round. In 1943, it took him only two rounds to repeat the feat. But Nova fought on for two years, during which he lost only three of his twenty-four fights. Thirteen of those victories were by knockouts. His last match was in Boston, where Tami Mauriello KO'd him in the first round.

He is still an enthusiastic boxing fan and is proud of his ring career. "I got out before my brains were scrambled," he said recently. "And no one ever said I didn't fight clean." Joe Olmos, chief inspector of the California Athletic Commission, agrees. Says Olmos: "For his time he was an excellent boxer. Today, he'd be considered great. But in those days there were so many good boys. He never stepped into a ring that he didn't give a good account of himself. Lou had style, ability and heart. He is a credit to his sport."

Since hanging up his gloves, Nova has been a sports columnist, lecturer, stand-up comic, poet and actor. In 1956, he conducted a recital of his poetry in Carnegie Hall. He has appeared in many plays, three of which ran on Broadway. Among his twenty-eight movies are *Joe Palooka, Champ* (1946), *The Leather Saint* (1956) and *Thoroughly Modern Millie* (1967).

The Guinness Book of World Records is considering his claim that he has entertained more people in more different ways than any other individual.

He has no children and is now divorced. When not on the road, he lives in Los Angeles.

When asked recently about what motivated his career in the ring, he replied: "I've often wondered myself. God knows no one ever encouraged me to box or do anything else. My dad passed away when I was six, and my mother was against everything I ever did or wanted. Maybe it was all those beatings she gave me when I was a kid. None of the guys I fought ever whipped me like she used to."

His mother is still living. According to Lou, "She's still mean as Hell. People think I'm awful for saying a thing like that but, believe me, not all mothers are what they're made out to be."

The man whom the late Frank Fay dubbed "a gentleman of wit" made the papers again in 1973 with his offer to fight any woman alive for a $100,000 purse.

He is unmarried and lives in Los Angeles. The former pugilist is a popular after-dinner speaker. (Joel Preisler)

By 1950 Vera-Ellen was one of MGM's most promising young stars.

VERA—ELLEN

The dancing star of movie musicals was born Vera-Ellen Westmeyr Rohe in Cincinnati, Ohio, on February 16. She has always said that her unusual, hyphenated name came to her mother in a dream. Her year of birth is usually given as 1926, which would make her thirteen years old when she debuted on Broadway. She was an only child and somewhat frail. Her parents sent her to dancing school when she was in the fourth grade because they felt exercise would build her up.

While still in her teens, Vera-Ellen visited New York City for a dance convention. She became a contestant on a popular radio program of the time, *Major Bowes and His Original Amateur Hour*. Her tap routine brought the most applause, and she was awarded the prize—a tour of presentation houses in several cities for a salary of $50.00 a week.

She and Gene Kelly were reunited for *On the Town* (1949).

Peter Lawford was with her in this studio publicity still of 1950.

Her first steady job was as a member of the Rockettes, who were then dancing at the Roxy Theatre. After a short stint with the late Ted Lewis' band, she was in *Very Warm For May* (1939). In that Jerome Kern-Oscar Hammerstein musical, she had one line which consisted of three words. Her next show was *Higher and Higher* (1940), which was followed by *Panama Hattie* (1940) and then with *By Jupiter* (1942). Along the way she picked up some encouraging personal notices and the nod of approval from the impresario John Murray Anderson. His name for her was "Seabiscuit." "Because," he said, "she's a winner."

Finally in *A Connecticut Yankee* (1943), she got two numbers in which she sang and danced. The late movie producer Samuel Goldwyn brought her to Hollywood from that show to play opposite Danny Kaye in *Wonder Man* (1945). They were teamed again in *The Kid From Brooklyn* (1946). Darryl Zanuck (retired and living in Palm Springs) borrowed her for *Three Little Girls in Blue* (1946) and *Carnival in Costa Rica* (1947).

The first time she danced with Fred Astaire was in *Three Little Words* (1950). Red Skelton was one of the other stars in the musical.

It was at MGM that she did her best work, though. The studio paired her with Gene Kelly in *Words and Music* (1948), in which they danced "Slaughter on Tenth Avenue." In *On the Town* (1949), she was with him, again. For *Three Little Words* (1950) and *The Belle of New York* (1952), she had Fred Astaire as her partner. In *Call Me Madam* (1953), she danced with Donald O'Connor. Although no mention was made of it at the time, her singing in movies was always dubbed.

White Christmas (1954) with Bing Crosby and Danny Kaye was her thirteenth picture. The same year she married Victor Rothschild, an oil man. Before coming to Hollywood, Vera-Ellen had been married to a young dancer. After her second marriage, she headlined in Las Vegas and made her last film, a flop called *Let's Be Happy* (1957).

In 1966, her wealthy husband sued for divorce, charging "cruelty." They had lost their only child shortly before in a crib death.

Although she has kept up with her dancing and dates occasionally, Vera-Ellen lives a quiet life in her hilltop house in the Outpost section of Hollywood. She has politely but firmly turned down offers to appear in films and to tour in the road company of *No, No, Nanette.* She was conspicuous by her absence from the reunion of Metro stars at the party for *That's Entertainment* in 1974. One of her biggest fans, Mike Douglas, has asked her several times to guest on his TV show. Her explanation is always the same, "I just don't think I have anything to talk about right now."

Vera-Ellen and Astaire on the set of their picture *The Belle of New York* (1952).

MILESTONES

1926   Born February 16, in Cincinnati, Ohio

1936   Began taking dancing lessons

1939   Debuted on Broadway

1943   Got her big break in *A Connecticut Yankee*

1945   Debuted in movies opposite Danny Kaye

1948   Danced "Slaughter on Tenth Avenue" with Gene Kelly

1957   Made her last film, a flop

Now divorced, Vera-Ellen lives in a hilltop house in Hollywood. (Jon Virzi)

JOHN HOWARD

The actor who was publicized as "the American Ronald Colman" was born Jack Cox on April 14, 1913, in Cleveland, Ohio. He was an honor student and won scholarships in high school and college.

1938 was John's fourth year under contract to Paramount Pictures.

When his family was hard hit by the Depression, John began earning extra money by playing the piano over the local radio station WHK. He was studying at Western Reserve University when he joined a cast of students in a dramatic reading of *John Brown's Body*. A studio talent scout approached him about a screen test, but Howard thought it was a joke and brushed him off. Then he got a call from Paramount Pictures with an offer of a contract beginning at $75.00 a week.

Howard began a seven-year association with Paramount in September of 1934. He debuted in *Car 99* (1935). The following year he was in one of the great tearjerkers of all time, *Valiant is the Word for Carrie*, which starred Gladys George.

Ronald Colman's portrayal of "Bulldog Drummond" had made the character a popular one with movie fans. Paramount had John grow a mustache and starred him in a number features playing the famed sleuth. Howard was able to project a certain intelligence, but audiences still thought of Colman as the authentic "Drummond."

Howard played the detective "Bulldog Drummond" in several movies.

He was opposite the late Arline Judge in the tearjerker *Valiant is the Word for Carrie* (1936).

Most of his many films were programmers: *Prison Farm* (1938) with the late Shirley Ross, *The Mad Doctor* (1941), *The Isle of Missing Men* (1942) and *I, Jane Doe* (1948) with Vera Hruba Ralston[4] (Mrs. Charles L. Alva of Santa Barbara).

In a recent interview, John summed up his career thusly: "If it hadn't been for Frank Capra and George Cukor, I would be remembered only as the man who made love to *The Invisible*

Woman." He was loaned out for Capra's *Lost Horizon* (1937) and for Cukor's *The Philadelphia Story* (1940) only because those two directors asked for him. At the time, Howard strongly objected to his parts in both pictures. Although he is glad he played in them, he feels both roles were weak, foolish men. The only part he ever really wanted was in *Gone With the Wind.* It went to Leslie Howard. He thinks his best work was in *Dr. Hudson's Secret Journal,* an exceptionally well-written TV series that ran from 1955 to 1957.

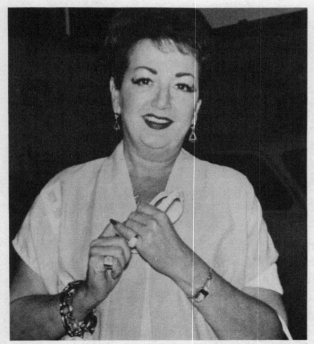

Arline Judge was as well known for her seven marriages as for her films. This photo was taken shortly before her death on February 7, 1974. (Jon Virzi)

He won a Navy Cross in World War II and then went under contract to 20th Century-Fox. He secured his release to do the musical *Hazel Flagg* (1953) on Broadway. He has done little since in Hollywood except *The High and The Mighty* (1954).

Howard lives with his wife and two children in the Brentwood section of Los Angeles. When he was hired away from his studies, he intended to save his studio salary and go back to school. Thirty years later he did. He now teaches drama and English at a private high school in the San Fernando Valley.

HIGHLIGHTS

1913   Born on April 14, in Cleveland, Ohio

1934   Signs seven-year contract with Paramount Pictures

1935   Is seen in his first film

1937   Appears in *Lost Horizon*

1940   Is in *Philadelphia Story*

1953   Has lead in *Hazel Flagg* on Broadway

1955-57   Stars in TV series *Dr. Hudson's Secret Journal*

John Howard today is teaching in a private school in the San Fernando Valley. (Glen Roven)

"THE STORY OF MARY MARLIN"

On October 2, 1934, one of radio's noblest heroines debuted over WMAQ in Chicago. "Mary's" trials and tribulations lasted on the networks through eleven seasons. For all her years on the air, including her revival over ABC Radio in 1951 and 1952, the show's theme was "Clair de Lune."

Jane Crusinberry (living now in Lake Geneva, Wisconsin) created and wrote *Mary Marlin,* which was touted as "a true-to-life story." Actually, it was less farfetched than most of the soap operas of its day and provided a vivid lead character with whom housewives could identify.

"Mary Marlin" went to Washington, D.C., as the wife of "Joe Marlin," the U.S. Senator from Iowa. She stuck by him through political and personal troubles that would have done in any ordinary person. Once he had amnesia. Another time, he was lost during a secret mission to the other end of the earth. She saw him through defeats and illinesses. But what hurt most was her suspicions that he was having an affair. The audience knew "Joe" philandered. In fact, regular listeners thought of him as "weak." When he was lost and presumed dead, many loyal fans felt "Mary" would make a much better Senator. So did Ms. Crusinberry, who put "Mary" in "Joe's" Senate seat.

Her solid and loyal friend was aptly named "David Post." "Mary" leaned on him in time of trouble, which was all the time. "David," who was played by the late Carlton Brickert, loved her. But then so did "Rufus Kane," the President of the United States, who went so far as to propose marriage.

The scheming socialite "Bunny Mitchell," who was played by Fran Carlon (living in Manhattan and still acting), had designs on "Mary's" husband. Another heavy was "Sally Gibbons," who was the first character in soap-opera history to announce for all Radioland to hear that she was pregnant out of wedlock. The character was played, at the time, by Anne Seymour.

Betty Lou Gerson, another of the actresses who played "Mary," with Don Ameche and the late Francis X. Bushman going over their scripts for a *First Nighter* broadcast in 1935.

Betty Lou Gerson is married and lives in a hillside house in Los Angeles. (Coleen Magee)

Several actresses played the lead role, including the late Joan Blaine and Betty Lou Gerson (living in Los Angeles). But Anne Seymour was "Mary" longest and brought to the part a very special quality. She projected an intelligence and earthiness that made the character very real to millions of listeners.

Ms. Seymour both acted and directed on radio as early as 1932. Her distinctive voice was heard on such radio programs as *Grand Hotel* and *The Magnificent Montague;* she had the title role of *A Woman of America.* On Broadway, she portrayed F.D.R.'s mother in *Sunrise at Campobello* (1958), and in the movies she was seen in *Man on Fire* (1957) and *Pollyanna* (1960). Recently, she has been seen on TV in such shows as *Marcus Welby, M.D.* and *Medical Center.* Her great uncle was the distinguished character actor Harry Davenport, and she is the godmother of Vincent Price's son. Anne is unmarried and lives in West Los Angeles.

Anne Seymour lives alone in West Los Angeles and is still very active in television and films. (Peter Cury)

"ROSIE THE RIVETER"

Peekskill's 'Rosie The Riveter' Sets Record

NORTH TARRYTOWN — Miss Rose Bonavita, twenty-one years old, of 224 Depew Street, Peekskill and Miss Jennie Fiorito, twenty-eight, of 10 Denny Street, Ossining, are believed to have set a record in riveting the entire trailing edge wing assembly of a Grumman Avenger torpedo bomber in the Eastern Aircraft Division plant of the General Motors Corporation in less than six hours.

The young women, who have been working as a team since November, drilled more than 900 lap joint holes, fitted the skins together and drove 3,345 rivets between midnight and 6 A.M. Naval inspectors approved the job without ordering any change.

Miss Bonavita and Miss Fiorito got permission to undertake the task, explaining that they were not trying to display their skill, but wanted to show what could be done in the way of assembling planes. Miss Fiorito formerly worked at the Fisher Body plant here and Miss Bonavita at the Highland Laundry.

Recently Rose received a letter from James Hickey, a boy friend, now on duty with the Navy in the South Pacific, asking for "planes and more planes." Suiting their action to the word, Rose and Jennie asked Foreman Joe Morabito for permission to attempt the staggering task of riveting an entire trailing edge section alone—and in one shift.

Miss Bonavita, the daughter of Mr. and Mrs. Anthony Bonavita, learned riveting at the Nyack Vocational School.

NEW YORK SUN,

ROSIE AND JENNIE SET RIVET RECORD

North Tarrytown, June 8.—A real life Rosie the Riveter, and her pal, Jennie, have set an industrial record at the Tarrytown plant of the Eastern Aircraft Division of General Motors, by riveting an entire trailing edge wing assembly for an Avenger torpedo bomber in less than six hours.

The girls are Rose Bonavita, 21 years old, of 224 Depew street, Peekskill, and Jennie Fiorito, 28, of 10 Denny street, Ossining, who began working as a riveting team last November. Recently Rose received a letter from her sailor boy friend, James Hickey, from the South Pacific, asking for "planes and more planes."

The pair asked permission to try the staggering task of riveting a whole trailing edge section alone in one shift, and they were given the chance. No one wanted to bet that they wouldn't finish the job, said Joe Morabito, the foreman. And they did finish it. "If we set a record," said Rose later, "we're sure happy about it."

"The record doesn't really mean anything," said Jennie. "The main thing, as we see it, is to get out as many wings as we possibly can."

'ROSIE, THE RIVETER' IN ACTION

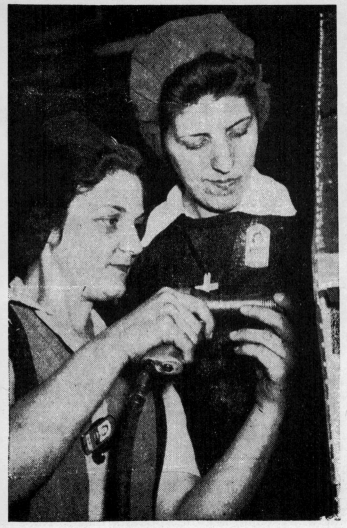

Rosie Bonavita, 21, of 224 Depew Street (right), and Jennie Fiorito, 28, of Ossining, demonstrate how they established a record at Eastern Aircraft at North Tarrytown, by drilling more than 900 holes, driving more than 3,345 rivets and thus completing an entire trailing edge wing assembly in less than six hours on a single shift. The assembly, for installation on Grumman "Avenger" torpedo bombers, was approved by Navy inspectors without a single bit of reworking.

Jane Frazee[4] played Rosie in the movie musical released in 1944. The late Vera Vague[5] took the role of her partner.

JANE FRAZEE · FRANK ALBERTSON · VERA VAGUE · FRANK JENKS · LLOYD CORRIGAN
MAUDE EBURNE · CARL "ALFALFA" SWITZER · ARTHUR LOFT

Rosie the RIVETER

A RE-RELEASE

A REPUBLIC PICTURE

JOSEPH SANTLEY Director

Screenplay by Jack Townley and Aleen Leslie · Based on the Saturday Evening Post Story "Room For Two" by Dorothy Cur

The defense worker who became nationally famous during World War II was born Rosina B. Bonavita on October 18, 1921, in Peekskill, New York.

In early June of 1943 at the height of the hostilities between the U.S. and the Axis, Rosie received a letter from her sailor-boy-friend who was serving in the South Pacific. It ended with, "If we only had more planes out here, we could lick the Japs-but quick." Rose showed it to her partner, Jennie Fiorito. The two were a team working the "graveyard shift" at the Eastern Aircraft Division of General Motors in Tarrytown, New York. It was a slow night. The pair went to their foreman, Mr. Morabito, and asked to try to assemble an entire wing of a Grumman *Avenger* torpedo bomber.

Between midnight and 6:00 AM, the women drilled 900 holes and drove 3,345 rivets-a record. Naval inspectors could not find a single flaw in their work.

Rosie has always maintained that it was Jennie who did most of the work. But when the story broke across the country, it was she who got the publicity. A song "Rosie the Riveter" made the *Hit Parade*. Republic pictures made a low-budget musical with the same title. She wasn't paid a cent for either. When the plant received the Army-Navy Production Award, the efforts of Rosie and her partner got special mention. President Roosevelt sent a personal message.

In 1944 Rosie married her sailor. After V-J Day in 1945, she left Eastern Aircraft and worked for a while in a canteen until her husband was discharged from the service.

Today, she and her husband, who is an electrician, live in Peekskill. They have three children. Once in a while, she hears from Jennie Fiorito, who resides in Florida.

Speaking recently of the work record that made her a household word over three decades ago, Rosie said: "It was such a different world then. Jennie and I were the same as all the people we knew. We worked hard because that's how we were brought up and because we believed in what our country was fighting for. We were very patriotic. Everyone was. I took a home-nursing course and gave blood many times. But you could never have made me do anything like that for the Viet Nam mess. For that I wouldn't have stapled papers, much less rivet steel."

Rosie is married to an electrician and lives in Peekskill, New York. (Jerald Mastroli)

THE HI-LO'S

The new sound of *The Hi-Lo's* was very much in evidence by 1955. From the top are: Bob Morse, Clark Burrows, Gene Puerling and Bob Strasen.

The innovative singing group was formed in 1953. Its arranger and leader, Gene Puerling, knew Bob Strasen from their native Milwaukee. Prior to *The Hi-Lo's*, they had been members of *The Encores*, a singing group with Billy May's band.

During the first six months, Bob Morse and Clark Burrows were added. This time was devoted exclusively to experimenting with sounds. They took standards which they modernized and improvised. The end result of their labors was certainly unique.

From an engagement at Fack's on San Francisco's Market Street, *The Hi-Lo's* clicked. They made a sudden and strong impact on the music world at the time, and their distinctive renditions are still much respected among fellow artists.

The Hi-Lo's cutting one of the albums they made during the 1950's. (William Claxton)

When their albums, such as *Suddenly It's The Hi-Lo's*, hit the market, they became particular favorites of the disc jockeys who gave them the amount of air play and personal plugs usually reserved for top recording stars. Sammy Davis wrote the liner notes on one of their albums, as did another fan, Jose Ferrer. Steve Allen wrote liner notes for them and featured the foursome on his popular network TV show five times.

They sang for thirty-nine weeks on television's *The Rosemary Clooney Show*, played the Brussels World's Fair in 1958, headlined at Birdland in New York City, won *Playboy's* Jazz Poll and were nominated for Grammies twice. Considering their media exposure, good reviews and the enthusiasm for their sound within the music business, their lack of commercial success is quite remarkable. With nine albums, all given continual air play, they never had one hit single record.

Bob Strasen has been an expeditor at the Jet Propulsion Lab in Pasadena since he left the group in 1960. Three years later, *The Hi-Lo's* broke up. Although he never sings, he and his wife often listen to his old recordings. He has two children and lives in La Crescenta.

Gene Puerling, who is married and lives in San Anselmo, California, has continued to sing, arrange and produce records. He has had three Grammy nominations for his work with other groups. He is presently part of a group that performs chiefly on commercials, *Singers Unlimited*. Another of its members is Don Shelton, who replaced Bob Strasen. He lives in Lake Forest, Illinois.

Bob Morse, who designed their clothes and album covers, has not sung a note since the *Hi-Lo's* disbanded. He is a partner in *The Two of Us*, a floral business in Costa Mesa, California.

Clark Burrows, a divorcé, lives in the hills of Sherman Oaks. He has arranged for *The Association* and is currently producing two rock groups. His former associates remember him as being on a continual "star trip." Says Morse, "If there was a complaint, he made it. If anyone was late, it was always Clark." Burrows' high notes were the most obvious individual contribution to their sound.

Morse is a florist in Costa Mesa, California. (Dick Lynch)

Burrows arranges and produces various musical groups in Hollywood.

None of the original members sees each other, nor do they make any effort to keep in touch. "We got along well," said one recently, "but we were never close friends."

Bob Morse summed up their curious professional history not long ago: "We were too ' in ' to break into the big money in those days. The pros loved us, but they only come to see you on opening night. Before the *Beatles* hit, we were considered by the general public to be too far out. Afterwards, we were passe."

Puerling, who was the leader and arranger is still very active in the music business.

Bob Strasen has been an expeditor at the Jet Propulsion Lab in Pasadena since he left the group in 1960. (Brian Gari)

MADGE EVANS

The child star of silents and popular ingenue of talkies was born Margherita Evans on July 1, 1909, in New York City. Before she was a year old, her mother, who had modeled before her marriage to an Englishman, launched her on a career.

Madge was on the cover of the fan magazine *Picture Play* in July of 1936.

Robert Young and Madge made three movies together in the early 1930's.

By the time of her Broadway debut in *The Highway of Life* (1914), Madge's face was already known to the public as "The Mellon's Food Baby." The same year, she played one of the Christian children being fed to the lions in the silent version of *The Sign of the Cross* and was the baby locked in the safe in the original *Alias Jimmy Valentine* (1914). Three years later, she supported Lionel and John Barrymore in the play *Peter Ibbetson*.

During her early career she was usually billed as "Baby Madge." One of her vehicles, *Heidi* (1921), was filmed in an early color process called Prizmacolor. She was so popular as a child in pictures that there was a line of clothing "For Little Ladies" that carried her name.

As a teenager, she made silents opposite

James Morrison in *On the Banks of the Wabash* (1923) and Richard Barthelmess in *Classmates* (1924). On Broadway she played a flapper in *Daisy Mayme* (1926) and was with Ina Claire[2] (living in San Francisco) in Somerset Maugham's *Our Betters* (1928).

Madge had been off the screen for seven years when Hollywood rediscovered her on Broadway in *Philip Goes Forth* (1931), a play by George Kelly (the uncle of Grace Kelly). She signed with Metro-Goldwyn-Mayer when they outbid Paramount for her services. Many felt M-G-M wanted her as a replacement for Anita Page,[5] who departed shortly after Ms. Evans arrived.

She played opposite Robert Montgomery in five talkies.

Una Merkel was with her in *Beauty For Sale* (1933).

Her studio certainly gave her enough exposure. In one year, 1934, she was seen in nine features. Nor did she lack for good company on the screen. She was cast opposite such established stars as Ramon Novarro, Charles Farrell, John Gilbert, William Haines and Al Jolson. Even when Madge made a programmer, Metro put her with promising newcomers like Robert Young, Robert Montgomery and Clark Gable. But by the time her contract expired in 1938, she had not become a star and had grown too mature for the ingenue roles for which she was best known.

In spite of the fact that her talkie career never really caught fire, she is fondly remembered, usually by men who were young at the time, as one of the loveliest blondes of that era.

Her movies include *Guilty Hands* (1931) with William Bakewell (now a Los Angeles realtor), *The Mayor of Hell* (1933), *Dinner at Eight* (1933), *What Every Woman Knows* (1934), *David Copperfield* (1935), *Transatlantic Tunnel* (1935), *Piccadilly Jim* (1936) and *Pennies From Heaven* (1936) with Edith Fellows.[5]

After leaving M-G-M she made only two pictures: *Sinners in Paradise* (1938) with Marion Martin (married to a physician and living in Santa Monica) and *Army Girl* (1938). Both were cheapies.

Una Merkel is single and lives in Los Angeles.
(Kristin Carole Rollain)

She returned to New York for the Philip Barry play *Here Come the Clowns* (1938). The following year Madge married the Pulitzer Prize-winning playwright Sidney Kingsley who wrote *Men in White, Detective Story* and *Darkness at Noon*. The couple share their 200-acre estate in Oakland, New Jersey, with their poodle, "Smoky." They have no children.

She does not rule out acting again although she recently admitted turning down an offer from Sidney Lumet; the movie director was one of the original cast of boys who appeared in her husband's hit play *Dead End*. Ms. Evans has also said that she would like to play in a film directed by Stanley Kubrick.

In *The Show-Off* (1934) Madge Evans was with Spencer Tracy.

Many of her early movies, including her first starring feature, *The Little Duchess* (1917), were made at Fort Lee, New Jersey. In those days, Fort Lee was the motion-picture center of America. Today, Madge and her husband are the main forces behind a movement to revive movie and TV production in their state.

For over thirty years Madge has been the wife of playwright Sidney Kingsley. (Jon Virzi)

DR. FRED C. SCHWARZ

The right-wing evangelist was born on January 15, 1913, in Brisbane, Australia. His father, who was Jewish, came to Australia from Vienna and became a lay Pentecostal preacher. After graduating from the University of Queensland in 1933, Schwarz taught high school and college. He received a degree in medicine and surgery in 1944 and then began a general practice in Sydney. Later he expanded into psychiatry and marriage counseling.

Schwarz first seriously became interested in Communism in 1940 when he fell into an impromptu debate with Max Julius, a leading Australian Marxist. After that, he read everything he could find on the subject, both pro and con.

The late Charles Edison (right), son of the inventor and a former governor of New Jersey, was one of those who appeared on the platform with Schwarz during his New York rally.

Dr. Schwarz set down his basic ideas in a book that was first published in 1960. It is still in print.

The doctor made his first U.S. lecture tour in 1950; it was sponsored by the controversial ex-minister the Rev. Carl McIntire and the late Dr. T.T. Shields.

In 1953, his Christian Anti-Communist Crusade was formed. Two years later, he closed his medical practice "so I could devote myself full time to the battle."

Pat O'Brien gave a dramatic reading of the national anthem at the Christian Anti-Communist Crusade rally held in the Hollywood Bowl in 1961. (U.P.I.)

In 1960, the basic ideas contained in his speeches reached the U.S. in book form, *You Can Trust the Communists (to be Communists)*. Still in print, its argument is that Marxists have been consistent in that they have never relented in their expressed determination to communize the world. Detente, non-aggression pacts and cultural exchanges are, in Schwarz's opinion, merely ploys to weaken capitalistic systems. "Peaceful coexistence is to a Communist merely a waiting period," says the doctor. "They take the long view and they mean to eventually dominate all of us. This has been stated by their leaders repeatedly. I've read them all from *Das Kapital* to the latest ideological newspaper from Peking."

The early '60's were the peak years for the Crusade. In 1961, 15,000 people packed the Hollywood Bowl to hear three hours of anti-Red revivalism. On the stage with Schwarz were Walter H. Judd, then a congressman from Minnesota (now living in Washington, D.C.), the late Senator Thomas Dodd and the publisher of LIFE, who made a public apology for his magazine's "misrepresentation of the Crusade." The event had the full support of the Hearst press and featured John Wayne, who led the Pledge of Allegiance to the flag. Pat O'Brien gave a dramatic reading of "The Star Spangled Banner." The proceedings were seen over thirty-three TV stations and were sponsored by Schick Razor and Richfield Oil.

Super star John Wayne led the Pledge of Allegiance to the flag at Schwarz's Hollywood rally, which drew 15,000 followers.

The atmosphere of the Crusade's 1961 New York City stand was described by TIME as "fervidly evangelical." Schwarz directed the five-day seminar that consisted of films, lectures and a banquet at a charge of $20.00 per person. It was announced that eight of his anti-Communist schools were then operating in the U.S. One published report had his organization's income from that year, after expenses, as $382,657.

The following year, he appeared on *Meet the Press* and opposed labor leader Harry Bridges in a heated public debate.

Schwarz has kept a rather low profile since that time. His organization sat out the politically turbulent mid-and-late '60's. The doctor does not believe in demonstrations. While his posture is very much the same, a few of his opinions have changed. In 1961, he spoke of the Peking-Moscow split as "just a product of our basic ignorance." Today, he accepts the schism as "very real and beyond the dialectical. Armed conflict, in my opinion, is quite possible." He was opposed to President Nixon's China trip.

Dr. Schwarz is still an Australian citizen and visits his homeland several times a year. All four of his children are doctors.

The Christian Anti-Communist Crusade has its headquarters in a large building in downtown Long Beach, California. The organization neither supports nor opposes any candidates; therefore, it is tax free. Its bi-monthly newsletter has 55,000 subscribers who pay $10.00 a year. Schwarz's latest book, *The Three Faces of Revolution,* is popular in right-wing circles.

Fred Schwarz the man is quite different from the dramatic speaker who still pleases conservative audiences all over the country. Although he has described himself as "a narrow-minded, Bible-believing Baptist," his manner in an interview situation is calm, objective and detached. He seems to have mellowed in the last decade; he told one journalist that he does not oppose socialism per se and would be comfortable living under a system such as Sweden's. Said the doctor, "I am a pathologist of Communism. I only provide information. I study and describe it as I would a disease."

Today the Crusade is headquartered in Long Beach, California. Schwarz is still its President and edits the bi-monthly newsletter which is sent to 55,000 subscribers. (Shelly Ramsdell)

NOREEN AND KEVIN CORCORAN

One of Noreen's early movies was *Plymouth Adventure* (1952).

There were eight children in the Corcoran family, and all acted in movies and on television. The two most prominent were Noreen, who was born in Quincy, Massachusetts, on October 20, and Kevin, who was born several years later in Santa Monica on June 10, 1945.

The Corcorans made their debuts in the 1951 version of *Show Boat*. M-G-M employees were encouraged to bring their kids to the set for a crowd scene in that picture. The Corcorans' father was the head of the studio's maintenance department. Kevin has no recollection of the incident, but Noreen says that she remembers it vividly and that she "just loved it. The whole idea of being in a movie was so exciting."

Noreen's big role was "Kelly Gregg" on the TV series *Bachelor Father*. On the show, which premiered over CBS in September of 1957, she played the niece of John Forsythe, who was the lawyer "Bentley Gregg." Her parents were supposed to have been killed in a car accident. Sammee Tong, who took the part of "Peter," their houseman, took his own life in 1965.

The situation comedy held its popularity through six seasons on the networks. Today, a plot that had a bachelor-about-town sharing the same house with a teenaged girl sounds like the script of an X-rated movie.

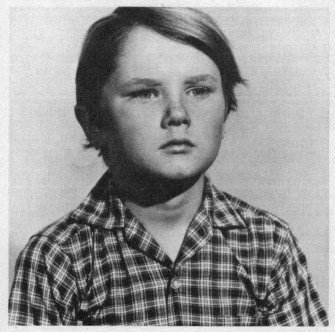

Many of Kevin's fans knew him only as "Moochie", the character he often played.

Dorothy McGuire,[5] Fess Parker and Tommy Kirk were in *Old Yeller* (1957) with Kevin.

After her series went off the air, Noreen had a running part on *Channing* and guested on such shows as *Dr. Kildare, Ben Casey* and *Gunsmoke.* She was in the features *Gidget Goes to Rome* (1963) and *Girls on the Beach* (1965). About the time of the movie *Blue* (1968), she began to tire of auditions, agents and other actors. "I enjoyed making *Bachelor Father,*" she said recently, "but I also knew that I was missing a lot of dances and dates because of it. Even when I had an evening free, there often was no boy. It's hard to meet boys on a TV set, and when you do, they often are insecure because you're a name." She also felt pressured about where she should or should not be seen and how she was expected to behave.

THE ZANY EXPERIENCES
OF A LADY COMIC
see page 20

LOCAL LISTINGS · JUNE 11-17

15¢

NOREEN CORCORAN,
JOHN FORSYTHE,
SAMMEE TONG OF
'BACHELOR FATHER'

When *Bachelor Father* went on the air Noreen was an awkward thirteen year old. By the time it ended she was portraying a pert young woman.

Noreen's dog on her TV series was named "Jasper"

Kevin spent eight years under contract to Walt Disney, making such pictures as *Violent Saturday*, non-Disney (1955), *The Shaggy Dog* (1959), *The Swiss Family Robinson* (1960) and *Bon Voyage* (1962). He played the character "Moochie" so often that many fans know him only by that name.

He says, "I quit acting because I just didn't like all the stuff that is involved in getting parts." Since 1972, he has been an assistant to a producer at his old studio. Kevin's wife is a secretary. They have no children.

Donna and Kerry Corcoran are housewives in Los Angeles. Kelly, who is the youngest, lives with his brother Bill, who is the oldest. Bill is married and lives in Fresno. Brian Corcoran is a security officer at a high school in Los Angeles. Hugh is a screenwriter.

Noreen has not been married. She shares a condominium with two of her brothers in Reseda, California. She is an executive with an acoustics-manufacturing firm. She is still recognized and says, "No one should ever feel shy about coming over to me if they'd like to. It doesn't happen often, anymore, but when it does, I enjoy it a whole lot."

Noreen shares a condominium with two of her brothers in Reseda, California. (Richard Schaeffer)

Kevin is an assistant to a producer at the Disney studios.
(Donna Schaeffer)

GLENN DAVIS
"Mr. Outside"

When this photo was taken in 1947 Glenn had just graduated from West Point and Elizabeth Taylor had just turned seventeen years old. (Wide World Photo)

The football hero was born on December 26, 1924, in Burbank, California. He was probably the most outstanding all-around athlete ever turned out by Southern California schools. While attending Bonita High School, he scored 237 points in his senior year playing halfback. He graduated with three varsity letters in football, three in track, three in basketball and four in baseball.

Glenn was offered an appointment to the Naval Academy but would not accept it unless they took his twin brother as well. When Navy turned down his request, he and his brother were quickly grabbed up by West Point. Ralph Davis never played football for Army. He is now a real-estate agent.

Davis made one movie. He was co-starred with "Doc" Blanchard.

For the next four years, Glenn's presence on West Point's team made life miserable not only for Navy but also for just about everyone else Army played. From 1943 until 1946, Davis carried the ball an average of 8.23 times a season. His rushing-yards averaged 1,028. As a receiver, he averaged 856 passing-yards. He made fifty-nine touchdowns.

In his second year at West Point, he took the Walter Camp Award and was named All-American. In 1945, he was chosen Outstanding

Player of the Year by the Helms Foundation and was again an All-American. In his senior year, he was All-American and accepted what he feels is the greatest honor of his career—the Heisman Trophy.

Throughout his Army days, he was known as "Mr. Outside," complementing his close friend and teammate Felix "Doc" Blanchard, who was dubbed "Mr. Inside."

After they graduated, Davis and Blanchard sought a five-month annual leave of absence from the service to play for the San Francisco 49er's. General Maxwell Taylor secured Pentagon permission, but as soon as the press got wind of the favoritism being shown the pair, there was a great deal of criticism by fans and in Congress. The order was rescinded before it ever went into effect.

Glenn and "Doc" Blanchard were TIME magazine's cover story for November 12, 1945.

His 1951 marriage to movie star Terry Moore lasted one year.

Glenn served out the remaining three years of his enlistment and then signed on with the Los Angeles Rams. His professional career, however, was very disappointing owing to a serious knee injury. Ironically, it was the only one he ever received. It came not on the playing field but while he was making his only movie, *The Spirit of West Point* (1947).

Since leaving the Rams after the 1951 season, he has been with the Los Angeles *Times* in charge of their special events. He lives in North Hollywood with his wife and teenage son, who doesn't play football, but who is doing very well in track.

"Mr. Outside" and "Mr. Inside," who are both members of the Football Hall of Fame, still keep in touch. Blanchard retired recently from the Army and lives in Burnett, Texas.

Davis was one of the first of football's glamour boys, and he was known to millions who neither knew nor cared about sports. His frequent dates with the teenage Liz Taylor were well reported. Although the fan magazines at the time breathlessly reported their engagement, Glenn said recently, "It was all cooked up by press agents. We had a lot of good times together, but we were never engaged or even close to it." His first wife was movie star Terry Moore. Their marriage lasted a year.

"Mr. Outside" is now Director of Special Events for the Los Angeles *Times*. (Frank Christi)

LUCILLE BREMER

The luscious red-haired movie star was born in Amsterdam, New York, on February 21, 1923. She prefers her last name to be pronounced "Bray-mer."

When she was seven years old, Lucille begged her parents to send her to dancing school. Five years later, she joined the ballet of the Philadelphia Opera Company. At the age of 16, she became a Rockette.

She danced with Fred Astaire in *Yolanda and the Thief* and *Ziegfeld Follies*.

LIFE magazine's cover story for its March 25, 1946 issue was on Lucille.

MARCH 25, 1946 **10** CENTS
YEARLY SUBSCRIPTION $4.50

After learning the routines of the famed troupe, Lucille and some of the other girls from the Roxy Theatre were sent on a tour of Europe. Upon her return to the U.S., she was hired as a member of the chorus in *Panama Hattie* (1940). She also understudied Phyllis Brooks in that hit Broadway musical. She had a featured part in *Dancing in the Streets*, but the show closed during out-of-town tryouts.

Lucille's next engagement was at the Versailles, one of New York's smarter night clubs of the period. She was waiting to learn the results of a screen test that she had just made for Samuel Goldwyn when producer Arthur Freed and set designer Cedric Gibbons of MGM spotted her. Both studios made offers, but she decided on Metro.

Her movie career got off to such a promising start in the memorable *Meet Me in St. Louis* (1944) that her original contract was scrapped in favor of a much better one. She was then picked to dance with Fred Astaire in *Yolanda and the Thief.* Although it is now highly regarded by some film cultists, it was a box-office dud at the time it was released in 1945. To those interested in screen choreography, the Astaire-Bremer dancing in the "Coffee Time" number is an unsung classic. During 1946, she appeared in *Till the Clouds Roll By* and *Ziegfeld Follies.* In the latter, Lucille was again paired with Astaire. Their surrealistic "Limehouse Blues" number from that picture is still a dazzler.

For the screen test that resulted in Lucille being signed by MGM, a scene from *Dark Victory* was used. Although her physical resemblance to Betty Davis was noted at the time, it was not until the very end of her contract that any attempt was made to allow her to really act, which she much preferred to dancing. In her last feature made at the Culver City lot, *Dark Delusion* (1947), she was very effective in a dramatic part. Screen historian Charles Higham has compared her performance in *Ruthless* (1948) with those of Bette Davis and has said, "It is a tragedy that she did not succeed as an actress."

She was beautiful, talented and willing. What Lucille Bremer lacked, however, are, perhaps, the most essential skills in sustaining stardom: a skin thick enough to ignore the professional jealousies that surround any star and a gift for studio politics.

Many felt Lucille bore a resemblance to the young Bette Davis.

While making *Adventures of Casanova* (1948) with the late Arturo de Cordova, she met Abelardo Rodriguez, the son of the former provisional president of Mexico. After their marriage, her millionaire husband discouraged her from acting. Nearly all of their life together was spent on a huge estate in Mexico. She says that she never missed movies during those years in which she raised her two boys and two girls. The couple, though, divorced in 1971.

Ms. Bremer recently closed the dress shop she owned and operated in La Jolla, California. She intends to make a lengthy tour of Africa and then settle in or near Los Angeles. She never hears from anyone connected with Hollywood. Although she does not rule out working in films again, she admits that the thought "terrifies" her.

Asked recently whether she is recognized much, she replies, "Yes, whenever I look my worst!"

MILESTONES

1923 Born in Amsterdam, New York, February 21st

1939 Becomes a Rockette

1944 Makes movie debut in *Meet Me in St. Louis*

1948 Marries wealthy Mexican and retires from the screen

Until recently she owned and operated a dress shop in La Jolla, California. (Tommy Cooper)

PINKY TOMLIN

The bumptious bumpkin whose 1935-hit song made him an overnight sensation was born on September 9, 1907, in Eros, Arkansas.

He was brought up in Durant, Oklahoma, and attended the University of Oklahoma, majoring in music and geology. His classmates dubbed him "Pinky" because of his florid complexion and red hair. It was the height of the Depression and Pinky worked his way through school with his own dance band. Before graduating in 1935, he wrote a song, "The Object of My Affection," for his girl, who had been Miss Oklahoma of 1933. She and the other students liked it, but it wasn't until he arrived in Los Angeles that the song and Pinky took off.

Pinky doing his bumpkin routine in a 1937 publicity still.

Tomlin starred in several low-budget movies in the late 30's.

He got a job singing with Jimmy Grier's orchestra at the Biltmore Bowl. The very first night he sang his own song, it was clear that he had a winner. The tune's tempo was just enough faster than that of other songs to seem quite different to the dancers who were used to crooning. On the strength of his Biltmore success, he was booked into the Paramount Theatre, where he stayed for sixteen weeks. After the fourth week, he had his name in lights.

Tomlin signed an M-G-M contract at $1,000 a week. The studio saw him as a triple-threat talent—actor-comic, songwriter, and singer. He became a regular on Eddie Cantor's radio show. TIME profiled him, referring to his "jackass laughter and owlish solemnity."

"The Love Bug Will Bite You (If you don't watch out!)"
was another one of the hits he wrote.

THE LOVE BUG WILL BITE YOU
(If you don't watch out!)

words and music by...
★ PINKY TOMLIN
writer of
"THE OBJECT OF MY AFFECTION"
"WHAT'S THE REASON I'M NOT PLEASIN' YOU"

SANTLY BROS—JOY, Inc
MUSIC PUBLISHERS
1619 Broadway · New York City

Pinky wrote "Love is All," which Deanna
Durbin sang in her movie *It's a Date*. He also
scored his own pictures: *Paddy O'Day* (1936),
Thanks for Listening (1937) with Aileen
Pringle[2] (single and living in Manhattan) and
Down in 'Arkansaw' (1938).

Hit songs lasted much longer in popularity
in the 1930's than they do today, and "The

Object of My Affection" was a super-smash. Recently, ASCAP, the organization responsible for tabulating royalties for composers and lyricists, named the tune as one of the most frequently played songs in its forty-year history. Among his other hits were "What's the Reason I'm Not Pleasing You?" and "The Love Bug Will Get You (If You Don't Watch Out!)."

Pinky had his own radio program, a summer replacement, in 1937. With his band, he headlined New York's Roxy Theatre and toured presentation houses all over the country. He cut over 100 records in his heyday.

Tomlin was often compared to Kay Kyser.[5] There were similarities in their looks and personalities, but Pinky never made the money Kyser did. By 1950, he had to admit that it was all over for him. "I'm afraid," said Tomlin recently, "that my fame exceeded my income." He now has his own business developing and selling oil properties. Tomlin readily admits, however, that he would love to do a one-nighter now and then.

At the height of his fame, he was reported to be engaged to the luscious blonde Toby Wing (now a widow living in Miami). "It never went that far," he says, "but it did go pretty far." They still exchange Christmas cards. Mrs. Pinky Tomlin is the former Joanne Alcorn, who in 1933 was crowned Miss Oklahoma. It was she who inspired him to write his biggest hit, "The Object of My Affection."

Pinky and the object of his affection. In 1933 she was Miss Oklahoma. Today she is Mrs. Tomlin. (Peter Schaeffer)

DOROTHY SHAY

The singer who became nationally famous as "The Park Avenue Hillbillie" was born Dorothy Nell Sims on April 11 in Jacksonville, Florida.

Dorothy's father, who owned a chain of gas stations, and mother wanted her to make her debut. She chose instead to accept an offer from her uncle, Walter Sims, Mayor of Atlanta. He paid her tuition to the Pasadena Playhouse, where she went to study acting in 1939.

In 1951 "The Park Avenue Hillbillie" was on the list of the Best Dressed Women in America.

One of her albums of 78 rpm records sold over one million copies in 1947.

During a visit home, Dorothy sang "Summertime" and "St. Louis Blues" at Jacksonville's Roosevelt Hotel one night. She went over very well with the local audience. Immediately afterward, she told her family that she had decided to sing instead of act. Her uncle withdrew his financial support, and she began a period of rather lean years.

One of Dorothy's earliest and most loyal fans was the late Louella Parsons. The columnist predicted her success after she caught Ms. Shay's act at The House of Murphy, a popular Los Angeles restaurant, in 1941.

She was still doing little more than making a living in 1945 when an agent named Merrill

Jacobs gave her the title that put her over. Dorothy had just concluded an engagement in Akron, Ohio, where, according to her, "I bombed." Although, at the time, she had only one hillbilly song, "Uncle Fud," in her act, Jacobs billed her for a Cleveland engagement as "The Park Avenue Hillbillie." From there, she went into Ciro's in Hollywood, where she was an opening act for Carmen Cavallaro (living in Columbus, Ohio). After that, she always headlined.

A little over a year later, Dorothy cut a record album that sold over one million copies, an exceptional number for those days of 78 rpm's. She received featured billing as the songstress on the late Spike Jones' radio show and guested for big fees on other programs. Her career was moving so fast in 1947 that she insisted on taking a European vacation to escape the hectic pace.

Dorothy had movie offers but made only *Comin' Round the Mountain* (1951) with Abbott and Costello. The big money, her managers reasoned, was to be had elsewhere.

She had a warmth and humor that appealed to an audience once known in show business as "butter and egg men". They were prosperous and square. For over a decade they packed the large rooms of the nation's best known hotels to hear "The Park Avenue Hillbillie" sing her hits: "Sugar Plum Kisses," "The Vinegar Tree," and "Feudin' and Fightin'."

Dorothy has some regrets about her career, which slowed considerably as rock and roll came in. She had turned down an offer to step into the Ethel Merman role on Broadway in *Annie Get Your Gun* during the star's summer vacation. It was for the same reason—money—that she passed up a chance to play "Lorelei Lee" in *Gentlemen Prefer Blondes*. Dorothy says it was she who suggested Carol Channing for the part when she turned it down. "I decided to stay in the big clubs where I could make more money," Dorothy recalled recently. Now with some hindsight, she says, "I suppose it was a mistake. Now I want very much to act, but I'm still thought of as only a singer."

She does manage to get acting jobs from time to time. Ms. Shay has done small parts in Disney features and cameos on such TV shows as *Adam-12* and *Police Woman*.

Dorothy made one movie during her heyday. In it she was co-starred with Abbott and Costello.

Although she still plays an occasional club date, Dorothy concentrates more on composing than singing. She recently wrote "To be Loved," a love song about a middle-aged woman and a young man that she hopes Peggy Lee will record.

Since her eight-year marriage to an auto executive ended in a 1959 divorce, Dorothy has lived by herself in Westwood, California.

In a recent interview, Ms. Shay spoke in her slight drawl about the title that made her a fortune but held her back creatively: "When it was pinned on me, I went along with it although it really made no sense to me. I was not from Park Avenue, and I certainly didn't think of myself as a hillbilly. There were times that I found myself resenting it and the image it created. But now, listening to my old records, I can understand why it worked so well. There is something in my voice that seems to make people want to take off their shoes."

She still plays an occasional club date and does small roles on TV shows.

MR. AND MRS. NORTH

The radio sleuths debuted over the NBC Radio Network in December, 1942. The thirty-minute program remained a fixture on prime time for over a decade.

Originally, the sponsor was "Woodbury, the cold cream for softer skin and an even softer and lovelier you." During the last five years it was Colgate. The theme music was "The Way You Look Tonight."

Faithful listeners, who numbered in the millions, remember "Pam and Jerry North" as they were portrayed by Joseph Curtin and Alice Frost, who originated the parts. During its last year on radio, the title roles were taken over by Richard Denning and Barbara Britton, who were also on the TV version, which ran for two seasons.

"Jerry North" was a publisher by profession, but his hobby was crime—especially murder. Alice Frost brought a delightfully ding-a-ling quality to the part of "Pamela," his wife, who seemed constantly to be coming across dead bodies. One of "Pam's" regular lines was "Look out, Jerry. He's got a gun!"

The couple first appeared in the mystery novels written by Frances and Richard Lockridge. When *Mr. and Mrs. North* was made into a movie in 1942, they were played by the late Gracie Allen and William Post, Jr. (now a regular on the TV soap opera *The Edge of Night*).

Ms. Frost originated the title role on *Big Sister*.[4] She is the widow of the distinguished director Frank Tuttle. She lives in Studio City, California, and is active on TV and in feature films. From 1937 to 1947, Joseph Curtin was the leading man to the late Helen Menken on radio's *Second Husband*. When he left *Mr. and Mrs. North*, he joined his brothers in an insurance firm in Belmont, Massachusetts, where he still lives. His daughter is the actress Valerie Curtin.

At one point, the pair, who are still good friends, attempted to take over the rights to the characters, but they were beaten out by an executive with the advertising agency that handled the show.

Both critics and viewers have found the characterizations and plot lines of TV's *McMillan and Wife* strongly reminiscent of *Mr. and Mrs. North*.

Alice Frost holding one of her three Shih Tzus. She is a widow and lives in Studio City, California. (James Cury)

Curtin is now an insurance agent in Belmont, Massachusetts. (Jason McCormick)

MILLIE PERKINS

The girl who was catapulted to international fame when she was chosen to play Anne Frank was born on May 12, 1938, in Passaic, New Jersey. Her father was a captain in the merchant marine with a large family. In high school, she was a cheerleader and was voted "prettiest girl in the class."

The news that an unknown had been chosen to play the legendary Anne Frank in a movie resulted in an avalanche of publicity for Millie both in the U.S. and abroad.

Before she went to Hollywood Millie Perkins was a top New York fashion model.

When she was eighteen years old, Millie moved into a Greenwich Village apartment with her older sister. She worked briefly as a receptionist until someone suggested she model. She did well almost immediately and appeared on the covers of *Glamour* and *Vogue*.

In the fall of 1957, she was having lunch in a Manhattan restaurant when a casting director for 20th Century-Fox walked over to her table and asked whether she would like to audition for the title role in the movie version of *The Diary of Anne Frank*. Millie had never heard of the heroine of the modern classic and brushed him off. Several weeks later, another Fox executive saw her picture on the cover of *Seventeen* magazine and got in touch with her. Rather than miss out on a lucrative modeling session, she canceled that first interview with the studio at the last minute. When Millie finally met with Fox executives, she laughed at their offer of a contract beginning at $150 a week. She made more than that every day she modeled.

When they raised their offer to $500, she became more interested; but it was the late George Stevens who convinced her to make a screen test. She was flattered by the interest of such a prestigious director and very moved by the Frank Diary, which she read at his suggestion.

Ms. Perkins says that she did not enjoy making the picture or the feeling that she was the property of 20th Century-Fox. She was adamant in her refusal to go on dates that had been arranged by the studio's publicity department. It was felt that she was being "uncooperative."

The movie opened in 1959 at advanced prices and a reserved-seat policy. It got mixed reviews, but Millie's were particularly disappointing. Throughout the filming, the press carped that, unlike Anne Frank, Millie was neither Jewish nor European. Some said that she wasn't an actress either. During a world-wide publicity tour, Millie found the press in England especially hostile to her.

The girl who was picked over 10,224 others to play Anne Frank did little afterward. Fox refused to loan her out to other lots or for a

Broadway play, claiming that she was "very special." When they finally did relent, she was farmed out as the third lead in an Elvis Presley starrer, *Wild in the Country* (1961).

Dit is een foto, zoals ik me zou wensen, altijd zo te zijn. Dan had ik nog wel een kans om naar Holywood te komen.

Anne Frank.

10 Oct. 1942

{translation}
"This is a photo as I would wish myself to look all the time. Then I would maybe have a chance to come to Hollywood."
Anne Frank, 10 Oct. 1942

The book *The Diary of Anne Frank* sold in the millions and was made into a hit Broadway play. Millie was unfamiliar with both when she was cast in the screen version.

In 1960, she married Dean Stockwell (living in the Topanga Canyon). They appeared together on a *Wagon Train* episode on TV. Within two years, she had parted company with Stockwell and her studio.

Millie has two daughters by her second husband, Robert Thom. She was in the film he wrote, *Wild in the Streets* (1968). During the marriage, she took courses at UCLA and taught cooking to grammar-school students. After their separation in 1974, she had an affair with a movie sound man.

Millie and Richard Beymer in a tender moment from *The Diary of Anne Frank* (1959).

Millie and her children live in a bungalow in West Los Angeles. She attends classes several nights a week in T'ai Chi. She has made several low-budget films with her friend Jack Nicholson and has decided that she now enjoys picture-making.

Speaking recently of her odd career, she said: "All that happened to me seemed very unreal at the time, and now it is as though it was part of someone else's life. I guess I didn't know who I was then, but I was not the person the studio made me out to be. For the first time in my life, I think of myself as an actress and a darn good one. It took me until I was thirty to grow up, but it was worth the wait."

Richard Beymer is now a film maker. His picture *Innerview* won a prize at the 1974 Mannheim Film Festival.

Millie still considers herself an actress. She and her two daughters live in West Los Angeles. (Martin)

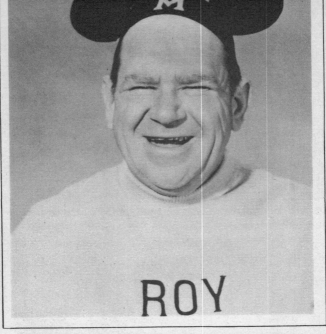

Roy invented and designed the "Mickey Mouse" ear hat.

ROY

"THE BIG MOOSEKETEER"
ROY WILLIAMS

The oldest and largest member of television's *The Mickey Mouse Club* was born in Coleville, Washington, on July 30, 1907.

Roy did especially well in art at the high school he attended in Los Angeles, Shortly after he was hired by Walt Disney in 1929, he enrolled for more training at the Chouinard Art School.

During World War II, he designed the insignia for the Flying Tigers, the Seabees and the P.T. mosquito boat.

With "Mouseketeer" Cubby O'Brien, who is now the drummer for the Carpenters.

Williams came into his own as "The Big Mooseketeer" in 1955. When *The Mickey Mouse Club* was still in the planning stage, Disney walked into Roy's office one day and said, "You're big and fat and funny-looking. You can draw cartoons on the show." Wearing the "Mickey Mouse" ear hat, which he invented and designed, "Big Roy" appeared on the program daily for the four seasons it was on the air.

Off-camera, he was its chief gag writer. "I loved every minute of it," he said recently. "I never grew up. I'm just a great big kid."

After production of the shows stopped in 1959, Roy traveled around the U.S. and Canada with his large easel as a good-will ambassador to promote Walt Disney movies. He continued as an animator at the studio until he reached the mandatory retirement age of sixty-five. Williams said recently, "I'm only a mirror reflecting the love and genius of Walt Disney."

Along with drawing cartoons on the show Williams was its chief gag writer.

He says he knew the series would be a big hit all over again when plans were announced for its revival in 1974. He is once again a celebrity to his one grandchild, as well as to all the kids in his neighborhood in Burbank. He has made his backyard into what looks like a set for a low-budget South Seas movie. Roy and his little friends enjoy the large pool and waterfall every day.

Williams both drinks and smokes, but he never permits himself to be photographed doing either. Nor will Roy permit anyone to publish the photo he keeps in his living room of his drawing a cartoon while a six-year-old Patty Hearst flirts with the camera.

His book *Vaporisms*, poems all on the theme of death, was published in 1967. A sample verse:

> "Hair keeps growing when you die;
> Hence the Hippies in the sky."

MILESTONES

1907   Born on July 30, in Coleville, Washington

1929   Hired as a cartoonist by Walt Disney

1955   Becomes "The Big Mooseketeer" on *The Mickey Mouse Club*

1959   Tours North America promoting Disney movies

1972   Is retired by Disney Studios

He is again a celebrity to the kids in his neighborhood in
Burbank, California.　　(James Cury)

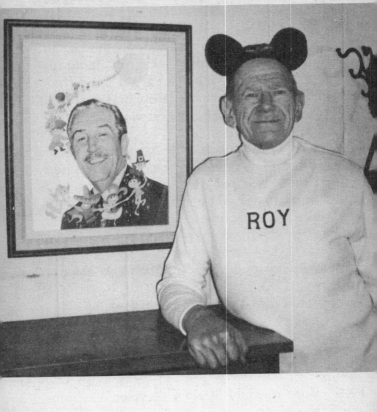

MARGARET LINDSAY

Margaret played the love interest "Nikki Porter" in seven of the *Ellery Queen* features made in the 1940's.

The queen of Warner Brothers "B" pictures was born on September 19, 1910, in Dubuque, Iowa. After graduating with honors from the American Academy of Dramatic Arts, she went to London. She was seen there in West End productions of *Escape, The Middle Watch*, and *Death Takes a Holiday.*

The story told about Margaret's Hollywood beginning, which she has never denied, is that she palmed herself off as an English actress. Her manner was sufficiently convincing that she got a small but important part in *Cavalcade* (1933). She played a young honeymooner in the "Titanic" sequence. It's a clever story except that Ms. Lindsay made several Hollywood pictures before *Cavalcade*, including the Tom Mix starrer *The Fourth Horseman* (1933). In any event, from *Cavalcade* she got the lead opposite William Powell in *Private Detective 62* (1933). Then she was the ingenue in *Voltaire* (1933) with George Arliss and Doris Kenyon.[4]

She was under contract to Warner Brothers throughout the 1930's. They used her frequently, but to no particular advantage. Among her many low-budget features were *West of Singapore* (1933) with the late Betty Compson,[2] *The Lady Consents* (1936), *When Were You Born?* (1938) with Jeffrey Lynn[5] and *The Under-Pup* (1939) with Gloria Jean.[4]

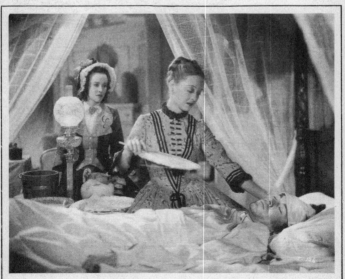

In 1938 she supported Bette Davis and Henry Fonda in the Civil War melodrama *Jezebel*.

A scar-faced Boris Karloff has the drop on Margaret in a scene from *British Intelligence* (1940).

When she was cast in "A" movies, they always starred someone else, such as Bette Davis or Jimmy Cagney.' The one high light of her career was for Universal in *The House of the Seven Gables* (1940). Although it didn't do much to boost her career at the time, it was cited recently by film historian Don Miller as "one of the great unsung performances." In it she runs the gamut from a vivacious young girl to a dried-up old maid. It was a beautifully shaded job with much depth.

Between 1940 and 1942, she played "Nikki Porter," the secretary-love interest, in seven "Ellery Queen" features at Columbia.

She was more selective about her roles once she began free-lancing, but she did not act often. Her later pictures were *The Spoilers* (1942), *Cass Timberlane* (1947), *The Bottom of the*

Bottle (1956), *Please Don't Eat the Daisies* (1960) and *Tammy and the Doctor* (1963).

The late Conrad Nagel and Ted Donaldson were with Margaret in *The Adventures of Rusty* (1945).

Ms. Lindsay's sister had a brief career as Jane Gilbert. Later, she married the late William Hopper, son of the gossip columnist. Margaret has always been close to her family. She has never married.

For a number of years, she was active socially in Hollywood, dating actor Richard Deacon and Liberace. Other intimate friends were Janet Gaynor and Mary McCarty. Lately, however, she has been seeing only old friends. She does not consider herself retired and was disappointed a few years ago when a TV pilot she made with Fred MacMurray did not sell.

She lives by herself above the Sunset Strip.

Conrad Nagel photographed just before his death on February 24, 1970.

Ted Donaldson works at the Pickwick Bookshop on Hollywood Blvd.

Margaret is still single. She lives alone above the Sunset Strip.   (Jon Virzi)

MILESTONES

1910 Born on September 19, in Dubuque, Iowa

1933 Had a key role in film *Cavalcade*

1940 Gave best performance in *The House of Seven Gables*

1940-42 Played "Nikki Porter" in seven "Ellery Queen" features

1963 Made last important movie *Tammy and the Doctor*

"SERGEANT PRESTON OF THE YUKON"

Dick Simmons as "Sgt. Preston" with his dog "Yukon King". The pair filmed seventy-eight episodes for television between 1955 and 1958.

The character of the lone Royal Canadian Northwest Mounted Policeman had a long run on the ABC Radio Network before he was seen on TV. Several actors played the title role, including the late Brace Beemer, who also portrayed "The Lone Ranger" on radio. The program's director for many years was Al Hodge, who later played "Captain Video"⁴ on television.

Both the radio series and the seventy-eight half-hour episodes for TV had as their theme the stirring *Donna Diana Overture* by Von Reznicek. Although it was photographed in 35mm, the series was seen only in black and white originally. Now that they have been re-released for syndication, the color prints are shown. Almost all of the filming was done on location in Ashcroft, Colorado.

Richard Simmons played the title role of the stalwart "Sgt. Preston" and directed some of the programs. His horse was "Rex." The show's other star was a beautiful Malemute Husky named "Yukon King."

The action-packed series was essentially the same on TV as it had been on radio, where it was called *Challenge of the Yukon.* In those days it emanated from the studios of WXYZ in Detroit, as did *The Lone Ranger* and *The Green Hornet.* Those two, as was *Preston,* were created and owned by the late George Trendle.

The other two characters and "Preston" all seemed to have no personal life. In fact, Simmons had played him for several months before he even knew what the character's first name was. It was "Frank," although that fact was never revealed on the air. There was never even a suggestion that he had any interest in women. Even more solitary than "The Lone Ranger" and "The Green Hornet," the Mountie did not have a close male companion like

"Tonto" or "Kato." His sole function was to
"enforce law and order in the frozen wilds."

The cover of the May-July, 1956 issue of the comic book
based on the adventures of the Mountie.

Simmons had spent fourteen years as an
M-G-M contract player before getting the role of
"Preston." He was first hired by Louis B. Mayer
and Howard Strickling, who spotted him at a
rodeo in Palm Springs. He was a commercial
pilot at the time. He has had gray hair since he
was nineteen years old.

When the series ended, he found himself typecast. Finally, he got another show, *Daring Venture*. During its filming, he was seriously injured in a helicopter crash in 1967. While convalescing, he studied real estate. He is now the managing director of a large community of expensive mobile homes in Carlsbad, California.

Simmons has happy memories of *Preston*. Although he no longer gets residuals, he is pleased that the shows are again being seen on TV. He is delighted with the fan mail, and he is again being recognized, mostly by the grandchildren of those who live at Rancho Carlsbad.

"Sergeant Preston" is especially well remembered by the thousands of fans who took advantage of a 1955 offer by its sponsor, Quaker Oats. The company subdivided a nineteen-acre tract of land on the Yukon River into one-inch plots and gave away deeds to delighted fans who wrote in. The public-relations office of the Quaker company replies to inquiries about the deeds with a form letter explaining that the land was repossessed by the Canadian government sometime ago for the nonpayment of $37.20 in taxes. According to the *National Enquirer*, one old fan intends to press the matter further. He is the owner of about 10,000 of those twenty-year-old certificates.

Simmons is now the Manager-Director of a mobile home community in Carlsbad, California.

"VAMPIRA"

The glamour ghoul of the 1950's was born Maila Nurmi on December 11, 1921, in Petsamo, Finland. Her uncle was the late Olympic champion Paavo Nurmi. She was brought to the United States as an infant and moved about for years with her father, a lecturer and writer.

In the 1950's "Vampira" was television's glamour ghoul. (U.P.I.)

Maila was brought to Hollywood by Howard Hawks who was going to launch her as "the new Lauren Bacall"

Howard Hawks found her in New York playing in Mike Todd's Grand Guignol midnight show *Spook Scandals*. The director brought her to Hollywood with the intention of launching her as "the new Lauren Bacall." Her debut was to be the film version of the Russian novel *Dreadful Hollow*. William Faulkner was engaged to write the screen-play. When the project was postponed again and again, Maila walked out on her contract.

She danced for several years for Earl Carroll and at the Florentine Gardens. At the latter, she was a chorine alongside Lili St. Cyr.[5]

"Vampira" in a personal appearance she made in 1954 at the Farmers' Market in Los Angeles.

Maila was married to screenwriter Dean Riesner (who acted in silent films with Charlie Chaplin under the name Dinky Dean, "The Boy's Boy") when she conceived the idea for "Vampira." She was at a costume ball when producer Hunt Stromberg, Jr., spotted her gotten up in a torn black train with shredded sleeves and bloody scratches just above her plunging neckline. Her waist, at the time, measured seventeen inches.

She was placed under contract to Channel 7 in Hollywood to host its 11:00 PM horror movies. The films were of such poor quality that Stromberg thought a weird and sexy lady would perk up viewers' interest. She talked of her pet spider, "Rollo," whom she could never seem to find and encouraged fans to write in "for epitaphs—not autographs." In a time of almost enforced blandness and conformity—the 1950's —she wandered through mist and cobwebs and made a sensation.

LIFE photographed her being driven around Hollywood by a chauffeur in an old, open Packard. She carried a large, black umbrella which she would put up on sunny days, "hoping for gloom." "Vampira" was never more macabre than when she walked past a panel of appalled but applauding celebrity judges as an entry in the Miss Rheingold contest. She was part of Liberace's Las Vegas act and made many guest appearances on TV shows. Orson Welles was one of her most enthusiastic fans.

Her act was unique and well done, but by the late 1950's she was no longer "hot." It all ended with her appearances in a few movies: *The Beat Generation* (1959) and *Sex Kittens Go to College* (1960). She believes that she is still a victim of an unspoken blacklist within the television industry.

She has remained in Hollywood through two brief marriages, both to actors. The woman who was so far ahead of her time with the gruesome characterization was also a step ahead of the nostalgia explosion. She was among the first to begin dealing in what was then called "campy junk." It is now referred to as "memorabilia" and she is a wholesaler.

Maila's star never set among Hollywood's underground, among which she is a legend. Her reputation for having known Jack Nicholson, Sally Kellerman and Dennis Hopper before they became famous is well-founded.

Her friendship with Marlon Brando goes back many years. But she has never exploited or capitalized on any of these relationships. She was very close to James Dean and has assisted several of his biographers. Maila denies that Dean was homosexual, but she confirms the rumors of his strong masochistic leanings.

An actor whom she befriended when he first arrived in Hollywood twenty years ago said of her recently: "Maila dyed her blonde hair black and wore half-inch fingernails. She used to smoke with a foot-long holder. But under all of that, she was goodhearted and very real." Those may have been the qualities that worked the most against her.

Maila is a legend to member of the Los Angeles underground. She shares her apartment with several stray animals. (Zeena La Vey)

Leonid played the bartender "Sascha" in the memorable picture *Casablanca* (1942).

LEONID KINSKEY

The Russian character actor was born in St. Petersburg on April 18, 1903. He performed as a mime with all three of the Imperial theatres before leaving his homeland in 1921.

Kinskey came to the United States via South America as a principal in the highly acclaimed Firebird Theatre. The company's failure at the box office on Broadway left him stranded in

New York City without money or a knowledge of English. Then Leonid managed to get a part in the silent film, *The Great Deception* (1926), starring Aileen Pringle[2] and Ben Lyon.[4] When he learned that his scenes had been almost completely lost in the editing, he accepted a position in Chicago, running a theatre-restaurant with a Russian theme. It was quite a success until the stock market crash of 1929.

Al Jolson hired him for the road tour of *Wonder Bar*, which brought Kinskey to Hollywood. Ernst Lubitsch caught him in the show and signed him for *Trouble in Paradise* (1932). The film due in part to his work in it is still rated as one of the classic comedies of the period.

Although he was never under contract to any studio, his Pinocchio nose and half-moon grin became famous for the hundreds of appearances they made in such pictures as: *Duck Soup* (1933), *Les Miserables* (1935), *The Road to Glory* (1936) with June Lang,[5] *The Great Waltz* (1938) with Miliza Korjus,[5] *I Married an Angel* (1942), *Monsieur Beaucaire* (1946) and *The Man With the Golden Arm* (1955).

Although he is usually remembered as "that crazy Russian," Kinskey's film credits show he had much more range as an actor than the image he left in the minds of most moviegoers. In *We Live Again* (1934) with Anna Sten,[1] he was a murder victim. In *Algiers* (1938), he played an oily informer. *So Ends Our Night* (1941) presented him as a sniveling coward. He gave a delightful performance in *On Your Toes*

(1939) as an eccentric and excitable composer. His most incongruous scene came in *Rhythm on the Range* (1936). Leonid harmonized with Bing Crosby, Martha Raye and Bob Burns in introducing the song "I'm an Old Cowhand." It is his personal favorite.

In his early lean years, he supplemented his income by writing articles and short stories for Russian language publications. During the Second World War, he began working with the Soviets in choosing Hollywood movies for showing in the USSR. He is still consulted. His countrymen and women, however, think he is an American acting the part of a Russian. Explains Leonid: "When I play Russians in movies they made me so exaggerated, no real Russian believed me." Kinskey is a U.S. citizen.

The late Joe E. Brown and Kinskey had a duet of "Sweet Adeline" in *Flirting with Fate* (1938).

He claims that *The Spot Lite Club*, a program he did over KTLA in Los Angeles in 1948, was the first situation comedy ever on TV. He was a regular on Jackie Cooper's TV series of the fifties, *The People's Choice*.

Today Kinskey writes and produces industrial shows. (Richard Schaeffer)

Kinskey, twice a widower because of cancer, has no children. He lives alone in North Hollywood. During the past twenty years, he was written and directed quite a few large industrial shows. He makes rare appearances on television but adamantly refuses to do commercials. He admitted recently that his interest in acting is almost dead. He did the pilot for the series *Hogan's Heroes* but then decided against signing for the series. Said Kinskey in his still heavy Russian accent: "The premise was to me both false and offensive. Nazis were seldom dumb and never funny."

HIGHLIGHTS

1903 Born on April 18, in St. Petersburg, Russia

1926 Makes movie debut

1931 Comes to Hollywood with Al Jolson. Is signed for *Trouble in Paradise*

1948 Makes TV debut with his own show

1956-58 Has regular part on TV series *The People's Choice.*

TOMMY KIRK

The star of Disney productions was born on December 10, 1941, in Louisville, Kentucky. When he was 15 months old, his family settled in Los Angeles.

Tommy's older brother, who wanted to be an actor himself, dared him to try out for a part at the Pasadena Playhouse. After landing that role, Tommy played on TV shows such as *Man Behind the Badge*, *Big Town* and *Matinee Theatre*. Then, from a screen test in 1956, he got the plum role in *The Hardy Boys*, a series that ran on *The Mickey Mouse Club* television show.

Kirk was placed under contract to Walt Disney in 1956.

With Annette in a scene from *The Misadventures of Merlin Jones* (1964).

Kirk seemed to be exactly the boy Disney wanted—at first. He had the features and manner with which family audiences identified. His pictures such as *Old Yeller* (1957), *The Shaggy Dog* (1959) and *The Swiss Family Robinson* (1960) were record grossers. But by the time he made *The Monkey's Uncle* (1965), the teenage star was a heavy user of amphetamines.

As early as 1961, while filming *Bon Voyage* (1962), Jane Wyman had made complaints about Tommy's behavior. On the same picture, Tommy received what he calls "the worst dressing-down of my life" from Fred MacMurray. "I really had it coming," confessed Kirk recently. "I was way out of line."

He was stunned when, after eight years under contract, the Disney Studios dropped him. Then, two days before he was to begin a role in *The Sons of Katie Elder* (1965), the police raided a party he was attending and found some marijuana. The charges were dropped, but so was Tommy from the cast of that John Wayne movie. The stories of his usage of drugs and alcohol were now all over Hollywood. Tommy's public image was almost intact, but the only ones willing to take a chance on his behavior were American-International Pictures and some independents.

Tim Considine played with Tommy in *The Shaggy Dog* (1959).

Tommy says he felt "very close" to Annette Funicello during the pictures they made together but they have not been in touch since then. She is now married to a Hollywood agent and has three children. (Richard Schaeffer)

He made *Pajama Party* (1964), *Ghost in the Invisible Bikini* (1966) and *Track of Thunder* (1968) with Ray Stricklyn (single and working as a press agent in Hollywood). His last ones, which he refers to as "grade Z," were *Mars Needs Women* (1966) and *Mother Goose a Go-Go* (1967) with Jacques Bergerac (now an executive with Revlon).

As Tommy struggled to stop using drugs, his attitude toward his career changed again and again. He did some summer stock and made a few TV appearances between stints as a waiter in Atlanta and as a janitor in Youngstown, Ohio.

The good notices he received when he acted in a play in Los Angeles in 1973 did not bring about a comeback. Kirk feels he has been "treated like a leper." He said recently that he thought "most people in this industry think I should go off somewhere and die quietly." His plans are less dramatic. During the same interview he said: "I want to watch a lot of people eat crow when I make it again. I'm not ready to work right now. I have to be a good person before I can be a good actor. At present, I'm concentrating all my time and energy on personal growth." He has given up both "speed" and drinking.

Today he is an active member of Los Angeles' gay church. (Blanche Taylor)

Kirk says he felt "very close" to Annette Funicello when they were making pictures together, but they have not been in touch since then.

Tommy is close to his family, although he says they hold very different points of view on many subjects. He is an active member of the Metropolitan Community Church, the largest gay congregation in Los Angeles.

Asked to sign an autograph recently, he half-smiled and wrote, "What will become of me?"

MILESTONES

1941—Born in Louisville, Kentucky, December 10th

1956—Landed important role on The Mickey Mouse Club

1961—Lack of personal discipline begins to interfere with his movie work

1964—Dropped by Walt Disney

1965—Arrested on pot charge. Loses important role although charge is dropped

VICTOR KILIAN

From 1935 to 1938 Kilian was under contract to Columbia Pictures.

The character actor who was blacklisted during the McCarthy era was born in Jersey City, New Jersey, on March 6, 1891. The youngest of eight children, he began working when he was 12 years old. Before he acted, he labored as a longshoreman, ditchdigger and brickmaker.

The first time Victor was on a stage was in Exeter, New Hampshire, in 1909. The play was a pirated version of a Broadway hit. Afterward, he toured the country in road shows and stock companies. For a while, he played in a vaudeville act called *Say It With Flowers*. One of the other actors in the sketch was Jimmy Cagney,[4] who got fired.

The original production of Eugene O'Neill's play *Desire Under the Elms* (1925) was in its ninth week when Kilian replaced one of the actors. It was his first time on Broadway.

Victor, the late Brian Donlevy and Kay Francis made their movie debuts together in *Gentlemen of the Press* (1929), which starred his close friend Walter Huston.

Victor supported Sally Eilers[4] and Donald Woods in the 1941 feature *I Was a Prisoner on Devil's Island*.

After doing *Valley Forge* (1934) on Broadway, he was signed up by Columbia Pictures. It was his only contract, and it lasted for three years.

Among his many films were *The Road to Glory* (1936) with June Lang,[5] *Tovarich* (1937), *The Adventures of Tom Sawyer* (1938), *Huckleberry Finn* (1939), *Young Tom Edison*

(1940), *Western Union* (1941), *This Gun For Hire* (1942), *The Ox-Bow Incident* (1943), *Spellbound* (1945), *Gentleman's Agreement* (1947) and *The Flame and the Arrow* (1950).

Kilian always preferred the stage to pictures, but he remained in Hollywood and made about six features a year until he found himself unhirable. Although he never testified before the House Un-American Activities Committee, he was one of the many who found themselves unacceptable to any major studio after 1951. It was six and one-half years before he got another job. When he finally was cast in a movie, the late Ward Bond made a great effort to get him fired.

In 1958, Victor returned to the stage when he replaced Hugh Griffith in *Look Homeward, Angel*. Two years later, he was again on Broadway in *All the Way Home*. His last play was *Gideon* (1961).

Kilian, a widower, lives by himself in a Hollywood apartment. He denies any bitterness about the blacklist.

When asked whether he sees any of the stars he worked with, he replied: "Stars and character actors do not mix socially in Hollywood. In New York I had close friendships with many stars, but in all the years I've lived here the only star who ever invited me to his home was Fredric March."

During a fight scene in *Reap the Wild Wind* (1942) with John Wayne, Victor lost an eye. Asked about the incident, he said: "It was not his fault, but I don't like him. Not for what he did but for the person he is." He calls the late

George Sanders: "The biggest snob I have ever known."

Victor's portrayal of "Grandpa Larkin" on TV's *Mary Hartman, Mary Hartman* has won him a whole new set of fans. Kilian plays "The Fernwood Flasher", a senior citizen who exposes himself to women in a small town.

Victor lives by himself in a Hollywood apartment.

(Richard Schaeffer)

LAUREN CHAPIN

Lauren played "Kathy," the youngest daughter of Robert Young, on *Father Knows Best* from 1954 to 1960.

The little actress who played "Kathy," the youngest daughter of Robert Young on the TV series *Father Knows Best*, was born in Los Angeles on May 23, 1945. When she was five years old, her parents were divorced.

Her mother, who Lauren says "had no life of her own," began taking her two sons around to casting offices. No sooner had she gotten their careers moving than she began pushing her only daughter. Michael, the older boy, drifted away from show business while in his teens. He now owns two Montessori schools. According to Lauren, Billy, the other brother, resented the fame she had during the six years she played "Kathy Anderson." The fact that the 203 programs, filmed between 1954 and 1960, are still among the most popular on television has kept him antagonistic toward her. They have had no contact with each other in years.

After the production ended, Lauren moved to Pasadena with her father and attended public school. She did a few parts on TV and was seriously considered for the title role in the picture *Lolita*, but the wholesome image her television series had created worked against her. When she was sixteen, she married a high school boy whom she later divorced. Her second marriage, when she was twenty, was annulled after six months.

"The Andersons of Springfield" were played by Jane Wyatt, Robert Young, Billy Gray, Lauren Chapin and Elinor Donahue. The show debuted over CBS-TV on October 3, 1954.

Lauren made a come-back attempt as a country-western singer, but her records didn't sell. She gave up acting in disgust after one producer offered her a role providing she go to bed with him and his wife.

The years 1966 to 1971 were, for Lauren, one long nightmare. She was physically and mentally unable to take care of herself. In 1971 after intensive analysis and therapy, she emerged from an institution and has been on her own ever since. She lives in Hollywood, using the surname of her last lover.

Until recently Lauren was a para-professional, doing lab work and counseling at a psychiatric clinic. With the help and encouragement of several friends she is again trying to make a come-back in Hollywood.

When she turned eighteen, $19,750, which by court order had been invested for her in savings bonds, was turned over to her. The remainder of the small fortune she earned on *Father Knows Best* was spent by her late mother, who was an alcoholic.

She is still friendly with Billy Gray,[4] whom she considers "family." Lauren has not seen Jane Wyatt or Elinor Donahue (still acting and married to TV producer Harry Ackerman) in many years. Robert Young, who played her dad, often called her "Kitten" on the shows. Although she has spoken with him only once since the series ended, she referred to him recently as "the warmest, dearest man I've ever known."

On one of the 203 programs, Robert Young's real daughter, Kathy Young (left), made her acting debut.

The center of her life today is her son Matthew, who was born in 1972. Asked if she would like him to model or act, she replied: "Once he's out of school he can do anything that makes him happy. But I want my boy to have a childhood, not the unreal, unhealthy life I was forced into. Kids should learn to relate to other kids—not to cameras."

Lauren and her son Matthew live in an apartment in Hollywood. She wants very much to act again. (Richard Schaeffer)

MILESTONES

1945 Born in Los Angeles on May 23rd

1954- Played "Kathy Anderson" on *Father*
60 *Knows Best*

1961 Married a high school boy

1965 Married again. After six months it was annulled

1966- Years of mental breakdown and ther-
71 apy

1972 Became a mother and began a career in psychotherapy

1975 Makes a try at a come-back

FRANKIE CARLE

Frankie's "Sunrise Serenade" was one of the country's biggest hits in 1939.

The pianist-composer was born Francis Carlone on March 25, 1905, in Providence, Rhode Island. He was one of nine children. Although he was interested only in sports, his mother was determined that he become a musician. When he was six years old, she insisted he choose the instrument he would most like to master. "I picked a piano," says Frankie, "because that was the biggest and most expensive, but they got me one anyway." He spent almost all of the money given him for lessons at the movies.

He made his debut at age nine with his uncle's band, and by thirteen he was writing songs. He took them from one publisher to another. They all liked his playing, but no one thought very much of his music.

In 1920, he went out for three years on a vaudeville tour with May Yohe. After that, he was with Edward J. McEnelly's Victor Recording Orchestra. By the time he left to join Mal Hallett's band, he was being featured. For the next three years, he shared honors with Jack Teagarden and Gene Krupa. Every date they played was a one-night stand, and in 1934 Frankie suffered a complete nervous breakdown.

Carle penned "Sunrise Serenade" in 1937, but it took him a year just to get someone to publish it. It took off right away, however, and his first royalty check was for $30,000. It has provided him with a handsome income ever since. Glenn Miller liked it so much he adopted it as his theme for a couple of years.

On July 13, 1939, with "Sunrise Serenade" No. 1 on the Hit Parade, Frankie joined Horace Heidt's *Pot O' Gold* radio show. Although he shared billing with Heidt,[2] he left to go on his own in 1943.

Frankie had several bands, and for five years employed his daughter, Marjorie Hughes, as his vocalist. He maintains that he was the first to have discovered the pint-sized pianist Frankie "Sugar Chile" Robinson[2] and Gordon MacRae, whom he found singing in the men's room at NBC. In 1942 and 1943, he was awarded *Orchestra World's* plaque as "The Nation's Outstanding Musician." In 1949, he was featured in the Doris Day starrer *My Dream is Yours*. The following year he had his second nervous collapse.

Frankie appeared on the sheet music of a song he recorded in 1950.

LET'S DO IT AGAIN

By DESMOND O'CONNOR and RAY HARTLEY

Recorded by
FRANKIE CARLE and his Orchestra on Victor Records

ROBBINS MUSIC CORPORATION
799 SEVENTH AVENUE • NEW YORK 19 • N. Y.

Frankie disbanded his last aggregation in 1957, although he still works, from time to time, at 1940's revival shows and on cruise ships. He and his wife of 50 years live in a condominium in Westlake Village, California.

Elyse Knox, Ross Hunter, Phil Regan and Phil Brito were the stars of a movie Frankie made in 1946. Hunter has since produced such films as *Imitation of Life* and *Thoroughly Modern Millie*. Phil Brito is an administrator with the city of Newark, New Jersey. In 1973 Phil Regan was sentenced to one to fourteen years in a California prison for attempted bribery of a state official.

He disclosed his formula for composing standards like "Oh, What It Seemed to Me" in a recent interview: "Ordinarily, I don't drink, but it seems the only way for me to write music is to get loaded. The night I wrote my biggest hit I got so drunk I worked all night. About dawn, just as I was finishing, the cops arrived. That's how it came to be called 'Sunrise Serenade.'"

Frankie wanted very much to sing as well as he wrote and played, but after three years of lessons, he had to give it up as a lost cause. But his real disappointment was not playing sports. He readily admits, "I would much rather have been a welterweight champion or big-league baseball player." The pride of his life right now is his grandson, who is the star athlete of his high school.

Elyse Knox, whose father was the Secretary of the Navy under President Roosevelt, married football hero Tom Harmon. Their daughter is married to singer Rick Nelson. The Harmons live in Los Angeles where Tom is a local sportscaster.

Carle today in the yard of his home in Westlake Village, California.   (Jason McCormick)

NASHUA

One of the great race horses of all time was born in the spring of 1952 at Claiborne Farm in Kentucky. The large bay colt with a star on his forehead was the product of the mating of the mare Segula, owned by the Belair Farm, and Nasrullah. Both horses had impeccable bloodlines. Segula was the great-granddaughter of Sir Gallahad II, who had topped American sire lists in 1930, 1933, 1934 and 1940. Nasrullah was also the parent of Noor, who broke many world records, and Never Say Die, the 1954 Epsom Derby winner. He had been owned by the late Aga Khan. Everyone expected their offspring to be a winner.

Nashua's strong personality which was evident almost from birth, seemed very glamorous to his public. Although Eddie Arcaro had some of his greatest victories astride the wonder horse, he never enjoyed riding him. (U.P.I.)

In his second appearance as a three-year-old, the star colt won the Flamingo Stakes at Hialeah Park by 1½ lengths on February 26, 1955. (Keeneland Library)

After being weaned, Nashua returned to the Belair Farm to be trained by the legendary James "Sunny Jim" Fitzsimmons. He had previously prepared for racing Nashua's maternal grandsire, Johnstown, who had taken quite a few honors on the track.

On his first time out, at Belmont Park on May 5, 1954, Nashua won by three lengths. After that, he won the Grand Union Hotel Stakes and the Hopeful Stakes. Then he came in second to Summer Tan, owned by Mrs. Russell Firestone. In that 1954 season, Nashua won six races and "placed" in the other two of the eight in which he was entered. He was named the Champion Two-Year-Old of 1954.

Nashua's strong personality was evident from the very beginning to his handlers and to the jockeys who rode him. Eddie Arcaro, who had some of his greatest victories astride Nashua, never enjoyed riding him. The temperament for which his bloodline was noted showed itself in his uncertain moods. To the public, however, it only added to the horse's glamour.

Nashua began his second season with a win at Hialeah, where he took the Spanish Moss Purse. He won the Flamingo Stakes a week later. Then he earned $100,000 for his owners at Gulfstream Park, where he won the Florida Derby. Ted Atkinson brought him in first in the Wood Memorial Stakes, in which he beat out Summer Tan, a top contender of his time, by a neck.

Nashua was the favorite to win the Kentucky Derby in 1955. He was expected to be the first horse to win racing's famed Triple Crown since Citation in 1948. Nashua, though, "placed" in the Derby that year; the winner was a horse from California, Swaps, who had not raced on the East Coast before the Derby. Nashua's rider, Arcaro, felt his horse was not in top form for the race.

Shortly afterwards, Nashua went on to win the remaining two jewels of the Triple Crown: the Preakness Stakes, where he gained a victory in which he shattered a thirty-year record for speed, and the Belmont Stakes, where he won by nine lengths. After that, he won the Dwyer Stakes at Aqueduct (by five lengths), the Arlington Classic and the Jockey Club Gold Cup (by five lengths).

Since both Nashua and Swaps had been un-beaten since their only meeting of the year, the Kentucky Derby, their owners and others felt a match race would be the best way to decide which horse was the better. Thirty thousand fans roared as Nashua, ridden by Eddie Arcaro, beat Swaps by six and a half lengths whose jockey was Willie Shoemaker, on August 31, 1955, at Washington Park. Nashua brought home the $100,000 winner-take-all prize. For excitement, drama and glamour, it is considered one of America's all-time great races.

A true wonder horse, Nashua had a full year in 1955. He was named the Champion Three-Year-Old and the Horse of the Year. His earnings were $752,550. It was, however, also the year in which his owner, William Woodward, Jr., was accidentally shot to death by his wife. Nashua was sold soon afterward to a syndicate headed by Leslie Combs, II of Spendthrift Farm in the first million-dollar transaction in horse-trading history. His exact price was $1,251,200.

With Eddie Arcaro his rider Nashua won a hard run race over a fast track at Belmont Park on October 13, 1956. It was a stunning victory by 2¼ lengths in the record-setting time of 3:20 2/5. (Keeneland Library)

Nashua opened his third season of racing in 1956 by winning the Widener Handicap by a head. But he was not even in the money at the Gulfstream Handicap, possibly because he was carrying 129 pounds, the most with which he had ever raced. Ted Atkinson then brought him in first two months later at the Jamaica Race Track. After that, he won the Camden Handicap at Garden State Park. By this time he had beaten Citation's record for purses and was the biggest money winner in racing history.

Eddie Arcaro had his third straight Gold Cup win riding Nashua in the 1956 Jockey Club contest. It was Nashua's swan song. He was retired from racing to become a breeder.

During his last season, Nashua had six wins and two unplaced starts. In his career he had won twenty-two times. Four times he had "placed." Once he "showed" and only three times did he finish out of the money. His total earnings during his three years of racing were $1,288,565.

Until recently, Nashua averaged between 32 to 34 matings a year for which his owners received huge sums. Among his offspring is Shuvee, a Triple Crown winner for fillies in 1969 and the world's leading money-winning thoroughbred mare.

Nashua resides in equestrial elegance at Spendthrift Farm in Lexington, Kentucky. He is no longer ridden by anyone. Age has not mellowed his personality. His groom, Clem Brooks, says he is still very much a horse with a mind of his own. Although few race horses even live to be as old as Nashua, the star thoroughbred still manages to mate with about twenty mares a season.

Nashua resides in equestrial elegance at Spendthrift Farm in Lexington. In spite of his advanced age the star thoroughbred still mates with about twenty mares a season. (The Blood-Horse)

"NO CRIME HAS BEEN COMMITTED"

Minutes before this photo was taken on August 31, 1955 Nashua had swept to victory over Swaps, another star racehorse of the period, for a purse of $100,000 at Washington Park. Nashua was then owned by socialites William Woodward, Jr. and his wife, the former Ann Eden. Mrs. Woodward had been known during her actress-model days as "the most beautiful girl in radio."

In the early morning of October 30, 1955 Mrs. Woodward fired a shotgun at her husband, killing him instantly. The grand jury that heard her testify that in the darkness she had mistaken him for a prowler ruled that "no crime has been committed." Woodward left an estate of $9,327,926.

Ann Woodward lived quietly after the killing in a Fifth Avenue duplex that had once belonged to the late fashion designer Hattie Carnegie. On October 10, 1975, almost twenty years to the day after the slaying, she was found dead. The Los Angeles *Times* called it "an apparent suicide."

JOHN KERR

John made his screen debut playing an emotionally disturbed young man in *The Cobweb* in 1955.

*To Richard Lamparski,
Best wishes,
John Kerr*

The stage and screen star was born in New York City on November 15, 1931. His mother was the late stage actress June Walker, who was "Lorelei Lee" in the original production of *Gentlemen Prefer Blondes*.

John was a student at Phillips Exeter when he began acting in stock. His first notable role was opposite Gertrude Lawrence in *O Mistress Mine* in 1948 at the Cape Playhouse. He became associated with the Brattle Theatre while at Harvard. His notices in the Brattle production of *Billy Budd* got him a featured part in

Bernardine (1952) on Broadway. Although its author, Mary Chase, wanted him fired, he received both the Drama Critics Award and a *Theatre World* citation for his performance.

In 1953, he played Jesse James to James Dean's Robert Ford on CBS-TV's *You Are There*. The same year he became a star as the boy troubled by his sexual identity in *Tea and Sympathy* on Broadway. "I got the part," says John, "because I looked exactly like the playwright, Robert Anderson. In fact, I am exactly like him. He's still my closest friend." He did the movie (1956) as well, again with Deborah Kerr. Their names are both pronounced "car."

John was very hot but only for a short time. When his agency, MCA, talked him out of doing *Friendly Persuasion*, the part went to Tony Perkins. If there hadn't been for some last-minute cast changes, he would have played Ensign Pulver in the movie *Mr. Roberts*. He turned down the part of Lindbergh in *The Spirit of St. Louis*, thinking it would be a flop. It was.

The Broadway production of *Tea and Sympathy* brought high praise for both John and Deborah Kerr. They repeated their roles in the movie version which suffered greatly from a changed ending.

French star Michele Morgan and John were teamed in
The Vintage in 1957.

His movies include: *Gaby* (1956), *The
Vintage* (1957) and *The Crowded Sky* (1960).
He was also the young officer who falls in love
with the native girl in the film-musical *South
Pacific* (1958).

By 1963, Ivy League types were well on their
way out. Kerr found himself doing a TV series,
Arrest and Trial, which he loathed. He even refused to test for the TV version of *The Green
Hornet* and began directing and lecturing on
theatre for ANTA. He was playing the district
attorney who prosecutes Ryan O'Neal on TV's

Peyton Place when he decided to become an attorney.

"It was an easy decision," he said recently. "I'd been around show business all my life and the glamour never impressed me. I deeply resented the insecure life of an actor."

He and Leslie Caron were in *Gaby* (1956).

In 1970, he passed his bar examination and now practices law in West Los Angeles. John lives with his teenage son. His wife got custody of their twin daughters when they were divorced.

Asked directly about a rumor that has circulated both in New York and Hollywood for years about his parentage, John shrugged it off with, "God knows how these things get started. My father was the playwright Geoffrey Kerr. My parents separated when I was a little boy; so, I never got to know him well." The story still persists that his father was the late Franchot Tone.

Kerr practices criminal law in West Los Angeles. (Michael Knowles)

In 1976 a nationally syndicated columnist reported that John was sharing a house with the widow of Wally Cox.

HIGHLIGHTS

1931   Born November 15th in New York City

1948   Debuted on stage with Gertrude Lawrence

1952   Debuted on Broadway in *Bernardine*

1953   Starred on Broadway in *Tea and Sympathy*

1958   Played in film version of *South Pacific*

1964   Left acting to study law

1970   Passed bar exam and began criminal practice

Tony Dow had no acting experience when he got the part of "Wally Cleaver." He had little to do on the shows, but his good looks made him many enthusiastic and loyal fans.

"LEAVE IT TO BEAVER"

Although Jerry Mathers[4] was the star of the long-running television series, almost as well remembered are Tony Dow, who played Mathers' older brother, "Wally Cleaver," and Ken Osmond, who was the troublemaker, "Eddie Haskell."

Dow had almost no acting experience when he accompanied a friend to the audition for the show's pilot. He canceled plans to move to

Hawaii with his family when he was chosen for the part. Tony was in almost all of the 234 half-hour episodes. In spite of the blandness of the role, he developed a large and loyal following among viewers attracted to good-looking high-school boys.

Ken Osmond was excellent as the conniving, two-faced neighbor. Most of "Beaver's" troubles were caused by this character, "Eddie Haskell."

The neighbor and nominal friend "Eddie" was the program's most colorful character. While always beautifully mannered toward "Mr. and Mrs. Cleaver," "Haskell" was the one usually responsible for getting "Beaver" or his brother or both into hot water. His name for "Beaver" was "squirt." He played a boy most people recall from their childhoods. He was scheming and two-faced, but, for the most part, his guilt went undiscovered and unpunished. Osmond had the perfect expressions and attitude for such a boy. It was an outstanding acting job by Ken, who has been a professional since he was very young.

Hugh Beaumont and Barbara Billingsley (both active in Los Angeles as actors) played "Beaver's" parents. The part of "Clarence 'Lumpy' Rutherford" was taken by Frank Banks (now partnered with his father in a catering business in Los Angeles). Another of "Beaver's" friends was "Gilbert," played by Lyle Talbot's son Stephen, who is now a newsman for Pacifica Radio in Berkeley, California.

Osmond and Dow felt comfortable in their roles and enjoyed filming the show. They and Mathers were close during its production, but when the three met at Jerry's wedding in the fall of 1974, it was for the first time in quite a while.

Dow is still recognized "about twice a day." After dropping out of acting for a few years to sail his boat, he settled down in a contracting business. A running part on *General Hospital* in late 1974 brought him back on TV. He has been married since 1969 and has one son. Asked recently whether being the show's sex symbol had helped him with girls, he replied, "Nothing helped me with girls. The only girl I ever impressed is the one I married."

Osmond is the father of two boys and lives in North Hollywood. Several times in the past few years, national publications have reported that Osmond had a new career in porno films. An actor who appears frequently in blue movies looks so much like him that even friends thought it was he. One movie theatre spelled out on its marquee: "Eddie Haskell of TV in 'Behind the Green Door' X-rated." The theatre's manager put up no argument when asked to remove the billing. The request came from Officer Ken Osmond of the Los Angeles Police Department's Vice Squad.

"Eddie Haskell" is now Officer Ken Osmond of the Los Angeles Police Department. With him is his son Eric. (Peaches Poland)

Tony lives with his wife and son Christopher in Van Nuys, California. (Michael Knowles)

INDEX

ABOUT THE AUTHOR

RICHARD LAMPARSKI is probably the world's foremost authority on the whereabouts of famous celebrities of yesteryear. He has based his selections for First Giant Edition of *Lamparski's Whatever Became Of . . . ?* on fan mail, phone calls and inquiries from readers all over the country, as well as the five previous editions of *Whatever Became Of . . . ?*. In addition to hosting his popular radio version of "Whatever Became Of . . . ?", Richard Lamparski has worked in television and radio as a public relations executive and as an associate producer.